OHIO

Contact

Dear Readers:

Every effort was made to make this the most accurate, informative, and easy-to-use guidebook on the planet. Any comments, suggestions, and/or corrections regarding this guide are welcome and should be sent to:

Outside America™
c/o Editorial Dept.
300 West Main St., Ste. A
Charlottesville, VA 22903
editorial@outside-america.com
www.outside-america.com

We'd love to hear from you so we can make future editions and future guides even better.

Thanks and happy trails!

Mountain Bike AMERICA™

OHIO

An Atlas of Ohio's Greatest
Off-Road Bicycle Rides

by Adam Vincent

The Globe Pequot Press

Guilford, Connecticut

Published by
The Globe Pequot Press
P.O. Box 480
Guilford, CT 06437
www.globe-pequot.com

Produced by
Beachway Press Publishing, Inc.
300 West Main St., Ste A
Charlottesville, VA 22903
www.beachway.com

Mountain Bike America is a trademark of Beachway Press
Publishing, Inc.

Editorial Assistance given by Sarah Torrey, Hee Jong Oh,
David Sarratt, Meredith Bosler, Lisa Gschwandtner

Cover Design   Beachway Press

Photographers Adam Vincent; photos in the Introduction
are credited to Scott Adams, Lizann Dunegan, and Adam
Vincent

Maps designed and produced by Beachway Press

Find Outside America™ at **www.outside-america.com**

*Cover Photo: OU cyclists tear it up at Dorr Run, near
Athens. Photo by Adam Vincent*

**Library of Congress Cataloging-in-Publication Data
is available.**

ISBN: 0-7627-0699-6

Manufactured in the United States of America
First Edition/First Printing

Acknowledgments

Though my name appears on the cover, this book wouldn't have been possible without the help of many different people.

First of all I would like to thank everyone at Beachway Press for making this possible. Your patience and direction are more than most writers can wish for.

I would also like to thank my mom, dad, and sister for encouraging me in this project and not asking "when is the book going to be done" too many times. The enthusiasm of my friends also helped keep me motivated.

Thank you Doug for being my regular travel companion and putting up with me getting lost all the time. Thanks Bill for your patience in Marietta—getting your truck stuck, driving around like the Dukes of Hazard trying to find our way to the trail, then getting caught in the mother of all thunderstorms. I also appreciated your help, Rick.

The Athens, OU Cycling crew were also of great assistance, making sure I had riding buddies and a place to crash after long nights at the Union and Tony's. Central Avenue is the place to be.

Scott and Lois Cowan, owners of Century Cycles and my former employers, were very understanding while I worked on this book. They gave me as much time as I needed to travel, and I'm sure they will buy lots of copies for the shop.

A big thanks also goes out to all of the private landowners who let me ride and write about the trails on their property. These are some of the hardest working people in mountain biking and have made some of the best trails and put on some of the best events in the country—not just Ohio.

Last, but not least, thanks to the readers for buying the book. I hope you find it the best guidebook out there. We have worked very hard to make it just that.

Table Of

Contents

Preface

ore than once, when I've told people that I am from Ohio, I hear the following: "I always thought of Ohio as this place that you drive through to get somewhere else." There was a time when I could see their point. I had never been out of my little corner of Northwest Ohio to see what else the state had to offer. And as a cyclist, I was convinced by the magazines and the media that all of the good riding was in California and Colorado. It wasn't until I began working on this book that I began to realize what Ohio has to offer.

The beauty of this state is subtle in many cases, admittedly not the billboard-drama of the Sierras or the Rockies. Beauty in Ohio can be found in little things like the sunset over perfect rows of corn or enchanting mists that form in the woods after rain storms. Or it can be the peaceful sound of a stream or river when you're used to the hum of computers and grinding of traffic. It can even be the smell of dirt and leaves as you faceplant over an unfamiliar drop-off. Other times the beauty of Ohio approaches the scenic drama of California and Colorado, like with the views of the cliffs along the Ohio River or the far-reaching rural landscapes seen from atop the hills of Scioto Trail State Forest.

Through researching this book I have discovered that beyond Ohio's beauty is an equally fascinating history, one that is closely tied to the fate of the entire United States. Ohio was the first frontier of America and had it not been conquered, the whole of the country may not have been settled. The stories of Ohio are as dramatic and violent (and certainly better) than most Hollywood movies.

And of course I wouldn't have discovered most of this if it weren't for my bike. I began riding off-road in Ohio when I was in elementary school. My friends and I would shred the trails behind my house, make the biggest jumps we thought we could land, and proceed to jump over each other. But it was more than just trying to prove that I was cool, that I could jump three of my friends and the wood pile. It gave me my sense of freedom—it would take me out of the neighborhood, to school, to the pool, to my first girlfriend's house, and anywhere else I wanted to go.

I gave up biking for awhile, but my first foray back onto the dirt gave me that old feeling of freedom once again. It was a wet, muddy day, and I was riding my brand new Raleigh. Although the bike had no suspension I loved the feeling of bombing down the slippery hill and almost landing in the river. I was hooked—again. Since that time I have upgraded to, and spent all my disposable income on, a lighter bike with suspension and more gears, and I now ride better trails, but the feeling of exhilaration is still the same.

More importantly, mountain biking has opened doors for me that would never have been available otherwise. I have met some of the best people in the world because of riding, traveled to some of the most beautiful places, and even found good jobs because of mountain biking.

My only hope with this book is that I can share with you the places I have seen and the things I have learned. I have done the research and gotten lost plenty of times so you won't have to. So learn about the state, do some great rides, and HAVE FUN!

Adam Vincent

A note from the folks behind this endeavor...

We at Outside America look at guidebook publishing a little differently. There's just no reason that a guidebook has to look like it was published out of your Uncle Ernie's woodshed. We just feel that guidebooks need to be both easy to use and nice to look at, and that takes an innovative approach to design. See, we want you to spend less time fumbling through your guidebook and more time enjoying the adventure at hand. So we hope you like what you see and enjoy the places we lead you. And most of all, we'd like to thank you for taking an adventure with us.

Happy Trails!

Introduction

Welcome to the new generation of bicycling! Indeed, the sport has evolved dramatically from the thin-tired, featherweight-frame days of old. The sleek geometry and lightweight frames of racing bicycles, still the heart and soul of bicycling worldwide, have lost much ground in recent years, unpaving the way for the mountain bike, which now accounts for the majority of all bicycle sales in the U.S. And with this change comes a new breed of cyclist, less concerned with smooth roads and long rides, who thrives in places once inaccessible to the mortal road bike.

The mountain bike, with its knobby tread and reinforced frame, takes cyclists to places once unheard of—down rugged mountain trails, through streams of rushing water, across the frozen Alaskan tundra, and even to work in the city. There seem to be few limits on what this fat-tired beast can do and where it can take us. Few obstacles stand in its way, few boundaries slow its progress. Except for one—its own success. If trail closure means little to you now, read on and discover how a trail can be here today and gone tomorrow. With so many new off-road cyclists taking to the trails each year, it's no wonder trail access hinges precariously between universal acceptance and complete termination. But a little work on your part can go a long way to preserving trail access for future use. Nothing is more crucial to the survival of mountain biking itself than to read the examples set forth in the following pages and practice their message. Then turn to the maps, pick out your favorite ride, and hit the dirt!

WHAT THIS BOOK IS ABOUT

Within these pages you will find everything you need to know about off-road bicycling in Ohio. This guidebook begins by exploring the fascinating history of the mountain bike itself, then goes on to discuss everything from the health benefits of off-road cycling to tips and techniques for bicycling over logs and up hills. Also included are the types of clothing to keep you comfortable and in style, essential equipment ideas to keep your rides smooth and trouble-free, and descriptions of off-road terrain to prepare you for the kinds of bumps and bounces you can expect to encounter. The major provisions of this book, though, are its unique perspectives on each ride, it detailed maps, and its relentless dedication to trail preservation.

Without open trails, the maps in this book are virtually useless. Cyclists must learn to be responsible for the trails they use and to share these trails with others. This guidebook addresses such issues as why trail use has become so controversial, what can be done to improve the image of mountain biking, how to have fun and ride responsibly, on-the-spot trail repair techniques, trail maintenance hotlines for each trail, and the worldwide-standard Rules of the Trail.

Each of the 30 rides is complete with maps, photos, trail descriptions and directions, local history, and a quick-reference ride information guide including such items as trail contact information, park schedules, fees/permits, local bike stores, dining, lodging, entertainment, alternative map resources and more. Also included at the end of each regional section is an "Honorable Mentions" list of alternative off-road rides (46 rides total).

1

It's important to note that mountain bike rides tend to take longer than road rides because the average speed is often much slower. Average speeds can vary from a climbing pace of three to four miles per hour to 12 to 13 miles per hour on flatter roads and trails. Keep this in mind when planning your trip.

MOUNTAIN BIKE BEGINNINGS

It seems the mountain bike, originally designed for lunatic adventurists bored with straight lines, clean clothes, and smooth tires, has become globally popular in as short a time as it would take to race down a mountain trail.

Like many things of a revolutionary nature, the mountain bike was born on the west coast. But unlike Rollerblades, purple hair, and the peace sign, the concept of the off-road bike cannot be credited solely to the imaginative Californians—they were just the first to make waves.

The design of the first off-road specific bike was based on the geometry of the old Schwinn Excelsior, a one-speed, camel-back cruiser with balloon tires. Joe Breeze was the creator behind it, and in 1977 he built 10 of these "Breezers" for himself and his Marin County, California, friends at $750 apiece—a bargain.

Breeze was a serious competitor in bicycle racing, placing 13th in the 1977 U.S. Road Racing National Championships. After races, he and friends would scour local bike shops hoping to find old bikes they could then restore.

It was the 1941 Schwinn Excelsior, for which Breeze paid just five dollars, that began to shape and change bicycling history forever. After taking the bike home, removing the fenders, oiling the chain, and pumping up the tires, Breeze hit the dirt. He loved it.

His inspiration, while forerunning, was not altogether unique. On the opposite end of the country, nearly 2,500 miles from Marin County, east coast bike bums were also growing restless. More and more old, beat-up clunkers were being restored and modified. These behemoths often weighed as much as 80 pounds and were so reinforced they seemed virtually indestructible. But rides that take just 40 minutes on today's 25-pound featherweights took the steel-toed-boot- and-blue-jean-clad bikers of the late 1970s and early 1980s nearly four hours to complete.

Not until 1981 was it possible to purchase a production mountain bike, but local retailers found these ungainly bicycles difficult to sell and rarely kept them in stock. By 1983, however, mountain bikes were no longer such a fringe item, and large bike manufacturers quickly jumped into the action, producing their own versions of the off-road bike. By the 1990s, the mountain bike had firmly established its place with bicyclists of nearly all ages and abilities, and now command nearly 90 percent of the U.S. bike market.

There are many reasons for the mountain bike's success in becoming the hottest two-wheeled vehicle in the nation. They are much friendlier to the cyclist than traditional road bikes because of their comfortable upright position and shock-absorbing fat tires. And because of the health-conscious, environmentalist movement of the late 1980s and 1990s, people are more activity minded and seek nature on a closer front than paved roads can allow. The mountain bike gives you these things and takes you far away from the daily grind—even if you're only minutes from the city.

MOUNTAIN BIKING INTO SHAPE

If your objective is to get in shape and lose weight, then you're on the right track, because mountain biking is one of the best ways to get started.

One way many of us have lost weight in this sport is the crash-and-burn-it-off method. Picture this: you're speeding uncontrollably down a vertical drop that you realize you shouldn't be on—only after it is too late. Your front wheel lodges into a rut and launches you through endless weeds, trees, and pointy rocks before coming to an abrupt halt in a puddle of thick mud. Surveying the damage, you discover, with the layers of skin, body parts, and lost confidence littering the trail above, that those unwanted pounds have been shed—*permanently*. Instant weight loss.

There is, of course, a more conventional (and quite a bit less painful) approach to losing weight and gaining fitness on a mountain bike. It's called the workout, and bicycles provide an ideal way to get physical. Take a look at some of the benefits associated with cycling.

Cycling helps you shed pounds without gimmicky diet fads or weight-loss programs. You can explore the countryside and burn nearly 10 to 16 calories per minute or close to 600 to 1,000 calories per hour. Moreover, it's a great way to spend an afternoon.

No less significant than the external and cosmetic changes of your body from riding are the internal changes taking place. Over time, cycling regularly will strengthen your heart as your body grows vast networks of new capillaries to carry blood to all those working muscles. This will, in turn, give your skin a healthier glow. The capacity of your lungs may increase up to 20 percent, and your resting heart rate will drop significantly. The Stanford University School of Medicine reports to the American Heart Association that people can reduce their risk of heart attack by nearly 64 percent if they can burn up to 2,000 calories per week. This is only two to three hours of bike riding!

Recommended for insomnia, hypertension, indigestion, anxiety, and even for recuperation from major heart attacks, bicycling can be an excellent cure-all as well as a great preventive. Cycling just a few hours per week can improve your figure and sleeping habits, give you greater resistance to illness, increase your energy levels, and provide feelings of accomplishment and heightened self-esteem.

BE SAFE—KNOW THE LAW

Occasionally, even the hard-core off-road cyclists will find they have no choice but to ride the pavement. When you are forced to hit the road, it's important for you to know and understand the rules.

Outlined below are a few of the common laws found in Ohio's Vehicle Code book.

- **Bicycles are legally classified as vehicles in Ohio.** This means that as a bicyclist, you are responsible for obeying the same rules of the road as a driver of a motor vehicle.
- **Bicyclists must ride with the traffic—NOT AGAINST IT!** Because bicycles are considered vehicles, you must ride your bicycle just as you would drive a car—with traffic. Only pedestrians should travel against the flow of traffic.
- **You must obey all traffic signs.** This includes stop signs and stoplights.

3

- **Always signal your turns.** Most drivers aren't expecting bicyclists to be on the roads, and many drivers would prefer that cyclists stay off the roads altogether. It's important, therefore, to clearly signal your intentions to motorists both in front and behind you.
- **Bicyclists are entitled to the same roads as cars (except controlled-access highways).** Unfortunately, cyclists are rarely given this consideration.
- **Be a responsible cyclist.** Do not abuse your rights to ride on open roads. Follow the rules and set a good example for all of us as you roll along.

THE MOUNTAIN BIKE CONTROVERSY

Are Off-Road Bicyclists Environmental Outlaws? Do We have the Right to Use Public Trails?
Mountain bikers have long endured the animosity of folks in the backcountry who complain about the consequences of off-road bicycling. Many people believe that the fat tires and knobby tread do unacceptable environmental damage and that our uncontrollable riding habits are a danger to animals and to other trail users. To the contrary, mountain bikes have no more environmental impact than hiking boots or horseshoes. This does not mean, however, that mountain bikes leave no imprint at all. Wherever man treads, there is an impact. By riding responsibly, though, it is possible to leave only a minimum impact—something we all must take care to achieve.

Unfortunately, it is often people of great influence who view the mountain bike as the environment's worst enemy. Consequently, we as mountain bike riders and environmentally concerned citizens must be educators, impressing upon others that we also deserve the right to use these trails. Our responsibilities as bicyclists are no more and no less than any other trail user. We must all take the soft-cycling approach and show that mountain bicyclists are not environmental outlaws.

ETIQUETTE OF MOUNTAIN BIKING

When discussing mountain biking etiquette, we are in essence discussing the soft-cycling approach. This term, as mentioned previously, describes the art of minimum-impact bicycling and should apply to both the physical and social dimensions of the sport. But make no mistake—it is possible to ride fast and furiously while maintaining the balance of soft-cycling. Here first are a few ways to minimize the physical impact of mountain bike riding.

- **Stay on the trail.** Don't ride around fallen trees or mud holes that block your path. Stop and cross over them. When you come to a vista overlooking a deep valley, don't ride off the trail for a better vantage point. Instead, leave the bike and walk to see the view. Riding off the trail may seem inconsequential when done only once, but soon someone else will follow, then others, and the cumulative results can be catastrophic. Each time you wander from the trail you begin creating a new path, adding one more scar to the earth's surface.
- **Do not disturb the soil.** Follow a line within the trail that will not disturb or damage the soil.
- **Do not ride over soft or wet trails.** After a rain shower or during the thawing sea-

4

son, trails will often resemble muddy, oozing swampland. The best thing to do is stay off the trails altogether. Realistically, however, we're all going to come across some muddy trails we cannot anticipate. Instead of blasting through each section of mud, which may seem both easier and more fun, lift the bike and walk past. Each time a cyclist rides through a soft or muddy section of trail, that part of the trail is permanently damaged. Regardless of the trail's conditions, though, remember always to go over the obstacles across the path, not around them. Stay on the trail.

- *Avoid trails that, for all but God, are considered impassable and impossible.* Don't take a leap of faith down a kamikaze descent on which you will be forced to lock your brakes and skid to the bottom, ripping the ground apart as you go.

Soft-cycling should apply to the social dimensions of the sport as well, since mountain bikers are not the only folks who use the trails. Hikers, equestrians, cross-country skiers, and other outdoors people use many of the same trails and can be easily spooked by a marauding mountain biker tearing through the trees. Be friendly in the forest and give ample warning of your approach.

- *Take out what you bring in.* Don't leave broken bike pieces and banana peels scattered along the trail.
- *Be aware of your surroundings.* Don't use popular hiking trails for race training.
- *Slow down!* Rocketing around blind corners is a sure way to ruin an unsuspecting hiker's day. Consider this—If you fly down a quick singletrack descent at 20 mph, then hit the brakes and slow down to only six mph to pass someone, you're still moving twice as fast as they are!

Like the trails we ride on, the social dimension of mountain biking is very fragile and must be cared for responsibly. We should not want to destroy another person's enjoyment of the outdoors. By riding in the backcountry with caution, control, and responsibility, our presence should be felt positively by other trail users. By adhering to these rules, trail riding—a privilege that can quickly be taken away—will continue to be ours to share.

TRAIL MAINTENANCE

Unfortunately, despite all of the preventive measures taken to avoid trail damage, we're still going to run into many trails requiring attention. Simply put, a lot of hikers, equestrians, and cyclists alike use the same trails—some wear and tear is unavoidable. But like your bike, if you want to use these trails for a long time to come, you must also maintain them.

Trail maintenance and restoration can be accomplished in a variety of ways. One way is for mountain bike clubs to combine efforts with other trail users (i.e. hikers and equestrians) and work closely with land managers to cut new trails or repair existing ones. This not only reinforces to others the commitment cyclists have in caring for and maintaining the land, but also breaks the ice that often separates cyclists from their fellow trailmates. Another good way to help out is to show up on a Saturday morning with a few riding buddies at your favorite off-road domain ready to work. With a good attitude, thick gloves, and the local land manager's supervision, trail repair is fun and very rewarding. It's important, of course, that you arrange a trail-repair outing with the local land manager before you start pounding shovels into the dirt. They can lead you to the most needy sections of trail and instruct you on what repairs should be done and how best to accomplish the task. Perhaps the most effective means of trail maintenance, though, can be done by yourself and while you're riding. Read on.

ON–THE–SPOT QUICK FIX

Most of us, when we're riding, have at one time or another come upon muddy trails or fallen trees blocking our path. We notice that over time the mud gets deeper and the trail gets wider as people go through or around the obstacles. We worry that the problem will become so severe and repairs too difficult that the trail's access may be threatened. We also know that our ambition to do anything about it is greatest at that moment, not after a hot shower and a plate of spaghetti. Here are a few on-the-spot quick fixes you can do that will hopefully correct a problem before it gets out of hand and get you back on your bike within minutes.

Muddy Trails. What do you do when trails develop huge mud holes destined for the EPA's Superfund status? The technique is called corduroying, and it works much like building a pontoon over the mud to support bikes, horses, or hikers as they cross. Corduroy (not the pants) is the term for roads made of logs laid down crosswise. Use small-and medium-sized sticks and lay them side by side across the trail until they cover the length of the muddy section (break the sticks to fit the width of the trail). Press them into the mud with your feet, then lay more on top if needed. Keep adding sticks until the trail is firm. Not only will you stay clean as you cross, but the sticks may soak up some of the water and help the puddle dry. This quick fix may last as long as one month before needing to be redone. And as time goes on, with new layers added to the trail, the soil will grow stronger, thicker, and more resistant to erosion. This whole process may take fewer than five minutes, and you can be on your way, knowing the trail behind you is in good repair.

Leaving the Trail. What do you do to keep cyclists from cutting corners and leaving the designated trail? The solution is much simpler than you may think. (No, don't hire an off-road police force.) Notice where people are leaving the trail and throw a pile of thick branches or brush along the path, or place logs across the opening to block the way through. There are probably dozens of subtle tricks like these that will manipulate people into staying on the designated trail. If executed well, no one will even notice that the thick branches scattered along the ground in the woods weren't always there. And most folks would probably rather take a moment to hop a log in the trail than get tangled in a web of branches.

Obstacle in the Way. If there are large obstacles blocking the trail, try and remove them or push them aside. If you cannot do this by yourself, call the trail maintenance hotline to speak with the land manager of that particular trail and see what can be done.

We must be willing to sweat for our trails in order to sweat on them. Police yourself and point out to others the significance of trail maintenance. "Sweat Equity," the rewards of continued land use won with a fair share of sweat, pays off when the trail is "up for review" by the land manager and he or she remembers the efforts made by trail-conscious mountain bikers.

RULES OF THE TRAIL

The International Mountain Bicycling Association (IMBA) has developed these guidelines to trail riding. These "Rules of the Trail" are accepted worldwide and will go a long way in keeping trails open. Please respect and follow these rules for everyone's sake.

1. **Ride only on open trails.** Respect trail and road closures (if you're not sure, ask a park or state official first), do not trespass on private property, and obtain permits or authorization if required. Federal and state wilderness areas are off-limits to cycling. Parks and state forests may also have certain trails closed to cycling.
2. **Leave no trace.** Be sensitive to the dirt beneath you. Even on open trails, you should not ride under conditions by which you will leave evidence of your passing, such as on certain soils or shortly after a rainfall. Be sure to observe the different types of soils and trails you're riding on, practicing minimum-impact cycling. Never ride off the trail, don't skid your tires, and be sure to bring out at least as much as you bring in.
3. **Control your bicycle!** Inattention for even one second can cause disaster for yourself or for others. Excessive speed frightens and can injure people, gives mountain biking a bad name, and can result in trail closures.
4. **Always yield.** Let others know you're coming well in advance (a friendly greeting is always good and often appreciated). Show your respect when passing others by slowing to walking speed or stopping altogether, especially in the presence of horses. Horses can be unpredictable, so be very careful. Anticipate that other trail users may be around corners or in blind spots.
5. **Never spook animals.** All animals are spooked by sudden movements, unannounced approaches, or loud noises. Give the animals extra room and time so they can adjust to you. Move slowly or dismount around animals. Running cattle and disturbing wild animals are serious offenses. Leave gates as you find them, or as marked.
6. **Plan ahead.** Know your equipment, your ability, and the area in which you are riding, and plan your trip accordingly. Be self-sufficient at all times, keep your bike in good repair, and carry necessary supplies for changes in weather or other conditions. You can help keep trails open by setting an example of responsible, courteous, and controlled mountain bike riding.
7. **Always wear a helmet when you ride.** For your own safety and protection, a helmet should be worn whenever you are riding your bike. You never know when a tree root or small rock will throw you the wrong way and send you tumbling.

Thousands of miles of dirt trails have been closed to mountain bicycling because of the irresponsible riding habits of just a few riders. Don't follow the example of these offending riders. Don't take away trail privileges from thousands of others who work hard each year to keep the backcountry avenues open to us all.

THE NECESSITIES OF CYCLING

When discussing the most important items to have on a bike ride, cyclists generally agree on the following four items.

Helmet. The reasons to wear a helmet should be obvious. Helmets are discussed in more detail in the *Be Safe—Wear Your Armor* section.

Water. Without it, cyclists may face dehydration, which may result in dizziness and fatigue. On a warm day, cyclists should drink at least one full bottle during every hour of riding. Remember, it's always good to drink before you feel thirsty—otherwise, it may be too late.

Cycling Shorts. These are necessary if you plan to ride your bike more than 20 to 30 minutes. Padded cycling shorts may be the only thing preventing your derriere from serious saddle soreness by ride's end. There are two types of cycling shorts you can buy. Touring shorts are good for people who don't want to look like they're wearing anatomically correct cellophane. These look like regular athletic shorts with pockets, but have built-in padding in the crotch area for protection from chafing and saddle sores. The more popular, traditional cycling shorts are made of skin-tight material, also with a padded crotch. Whichever style you find most comfortable, cycling shorts are a necessity for long rides.

Food. This essential item will keep you rolling. Cycling burns up a lot of calories and is among the few sports in which no one is safe from the "Bonk." Bonking feels like it sounds. Without food in your system, your blood sugar level collapses, and there is no longer any energy in your body. This instantly results in total fatigue and light-headedness. So when you're filling your water bottle, remember to bring along some food. Fruit, energy bars, or some other forms of high-energy food are highly recommended. Candy bars are not, however, because they will deliver a sudden burst of high energy, then let you down soon after, causing you to feel worse than before. Energy bars are available at most bike stores and are similar to candy bars, but provide complex carbohydrate energy and high nutrition rather than fast-burning simple sugars.

BE PREPARED OR DIE

Essential equipment that will keep you from dying alone in the woods:

- **Spare Tube**
- **Tire Irons**—See the Appendix for instructions on fixing flat tires.
- **Patch Kit**
- **Pump**
- **Money**—Spare change for emergency calls.

- **Spoke Wrench**
- **Spare Spokes**—To fit your wheel. Tape these to the chain stay.
- **Chain Tool**
- **Allen Keys**—Bring appropriate sizes to fit your bike.
- **Compass**
- **First-Aid Kit**
- **Rain Gear**—For quick changes in weather.
- **Matches**
- **Guidebook**—In case all else fails and you must start a fire to survive, this guide-book will serve as excellent fire starter!

To carry these items, you may need a bike bag. A bag mounted in front of the han-dlebars provides quick access to your belongings, whereas a saddle bag fitted under-neath the saddle keeps things out of your way. If you're carrying lots of equipment, you may want to consider a set of panniers. These are much larger and mount on either side of each wheel on a rack. Many cyclists, though, prefer not to use a bag at all. They just slip all they need into their jersey pockets, and off they go.

BE SAFE—WEAR YOUR ARMOR

While on the subject of jerseys, it's crucial to discuss the cloth-ing you must wear to be safe, practical, and—if you prefer—styl-ish. The following is a list of items that will save you from disas-ter, outfit you comfortably, and most important, keep you looking cool.

Helmet. A helmet is an absolute necessity because it protects your head from complete annihilation. It is the only thing that will not disintegrate into a million pieces after a wicked crash on a descent you shouldn't have been on in the first place. A helmet with a solid exterior shell will also protect your head from sharp or protruding objects. Of course, with a hard-shelled helmet, you can paste several stickers of your favorite bicycle manufacturers all over the outer shell, giving companies even more free advertising for your dollar.

Shorts. Let's just say Lycra™ cycling shorts are considered a major safety item if you plan to ride for more than 20 or 30 minutes at a time. As mentioned in *The Necessities of Cycling* section, cycling shorts are well regarded as the leading cure-all for chafing and saddle sores. The most preventive cycling shorts have padded "chamois" (most chamois is synthetic nowadays) in the crotch area. Of course, if you choose to wear these traditional cycling shorts, it's imperative that they look as if someone spray painted them onto your body.

Gloves. You may find well-padded cycling gloves invaluable when traveling over rocky trails and gravelly roads for hours on end. Long-fingered gloves may also be use-ful, as branches, trees, assorted hard objects, and, occasionally, small animals will reach out and whack your knuckles.

Glasses. Not only do sunglasses give you an imposing presence and make you look cool (both are extremely important), they also protect your eyes from harmful ultraviolet rays, invisible branches, creepy bugs, dirt, and may prevent you from being caught sneaking glances at riders of the opposite sex also wearing skintight, revealing Lycra™.

Shoes. Mountain bike shoes should have stiff soles to help make pedaling easier and provide better traction when walking your bike up a trail becomes necessary. Virtually any kind of good outdoor hiking footwear will work, but specific mountain bike shoes (especially those with inset cleats) are best. It is vital that these shoes look as ugly as humanly possible. Those closest in style to bowling shoes are, of course, the most popular.

Jersey or Shirt. Bicycling jerseys are popular because of their snug fit and back pockets. When purchasing a jersey, look for ones that are loaded with bright, blinding, neon logos and manufacturers' names. These loudly decorated billboards are also good for drawing unnecessary attention to yourself just before taking a mean spill while trying to hop a curb. A cotton T-shirt is a good alternative in warm weather, but when the weather turns cold, cotton becomes a chilling substitute for the jersey. Cotton retains moisture and sweat against your body, which may cause you to get the chills and ills on those cold-weather rides.

OH, THOSE COLD OHIO DAYS

If the weather chooses not to cooperate on the day you've set aside for a bike ride, it's helpful to be prepared.

Tights or leg warmers. These are best in temperatures below 55 degrees. Knees are sensitive and can develop all kinds of problems if they get cold. Common problems include tendinitis, bursitis, and arthritis.

Plenty of layers on your upper body. When the air has a nip in it, layers of clothing will keep the chill away from your chest and help prevent the development of bronchitis. If the air is cool, a Polypropylene™ or Capilene™ long-sleeved shirt is best to wear against the skin beneath other layers of clothing. Polypropylene or Capilene, like wool, wicks away moisture from your skin to keep your body dry. Try to avoid wearing cotton or baggy clothing when the temperature falls. Cotton, as mentioned before, holds moisture like a sponge, and baggy clothing catches cold air and swirls it around your body. Good cold-weather clothing should fit snugly against your body, but not be restrictive.

Wool socks. Don't pack too many layers under those shoes, though. You may stand the chance of restricting circulation, and your feet will get real cold, real fast.

Thinsulate or Gortex™ gloves. We may all agree that there is nothing worse than frozen feet—unless your hands are frozen. A good pair of Thinsulate™ or Gortex™ gloves should keep your hands toasty and warm.

Hat or helmet on cold days? Sometimes, when the weather gets really cold and you still want to hit the trails, it's tough to stay warm. We all know that 130 percent of the body's heat escapes through the head (overactive brains, I imagine), so it's important to keep the cranium warm. Ventilated helmets are designed to keep heads cool in the summer heat, but they do little to help keep heads warm during rides in sub-zero temperatures. Cyclists should consider wearing a hat on extremely cold days.

Capilene skullcaps are great head and ear warmers that snugly fit over your head beneath the helmet. Head protection is not lost. Another option is a helmet cover that covers those ventilating gaps and helps keep the body heat in. These do not, however, keep your ears warm. Some cyclists will opt for a simple knit cycling cap sans the helmet, but these have never been shown to be very good cranium protectors.

All of this clothing can be found at your local bike store, where the staff should be happy to help fit you into the seasons of the year.

TO HAVE OR NOT TO HAVE... *(Other Very Useful Items)*

Though mountain biking is relatively new to the cycling scene, there is no shortage of items for you and your bike to make riding better, safer, and easier. We have rummaged through the unending lists and separated the gadgets from the good stuff, coming up with what we believe are items certain to make mountain bike riding easier and more enjoyable.

Tires. Buying yourself a good pair of knobby tires is the quickest way to enhance the off-road handling capabilities of your bike. There are many types of mountain bike tires on the market. Some are made exclusively for very rugged off-road terrain. These big-knobbed, soft rubber tires virtually stick to the ground with unforgiving traction, but tend to deteriorate quickly on pavement. There are other tires made exclusively for the road. These are called "slicks" and have no tread at all. For the average cyclist, though, a good tire somewhere in the middle of these two extremes should do the trick.

Toe Clips or Clipless Pedals. With these, you will ride with more power. Toe clips attach to your pedals and strap your feet firmly in place, allowing you to exert pressure on the pedals on both the downstroke and the upstroke. They will increase your pedaling efficiency by 30 percent to 50 percent. Clipless pedals, which liberate your feet from the traditional straps and clips, have made toe clips virtually obsolete. Like ski bindings, they attach your shoe directly to the pedal. They are, however, much more expensive than toe clips.

Bar Ends. These great clamp-on additions to your original straight bar will provide more leverage, an excellent grip for climbing, and a more natural position for your hands. Be aware, however, of the bar end's propensity for hooking trees on fast descents, sending you, the cyclist, airborne.

Fanny Pack. These bags are ideal for carrying keys, extra food, guidebooks, tools, spare tubes, and a cellular phone, in case you need to call for help.

Suspension Forks. For the more serious off-roaders who want nothing to impede their speed on the trails, investing in a pair of suspension forks is a good idea. Like tires, there are plenty of brands to choose from, and they all do the same thing—absorb the brutal beatings of a rough trail. The cost of these forks, however, is sometimes more brutal than the trail itself.

Bike Computers. These are fun gadgets to own and are much less expensive than in years past. They have such features as trip distance, speedometer, odometer, time of day, altitude, alarm, average speed, maximum speed, heart rate, global satellite positioning, etc. Bike computers will come in handy when following these maps or to know just how far you've ridden in the wrong direction.

Water Pack. This is quickly becoming an essential item for cyclists pedaling for more than a few hours, especially in hot, dry conditions. The most popular brand is, of course, the Camelback™, and these water packs can carry in their bladder bags as much as 100 ounces of water. These packs strap onto your back with a handy hose running over your shoulder so you can be drinking water while still holding onto the bars on a rocky descent with both hands. These packs are a great way to carry a lot of extra liquid on hot rides in the middle of nowhere.

TYPES OF OFF-ROAD TERRAIN

Before roughing it off road, we may first have to ride the pavement to get to our destination. Please, don't be dismayed. Some of the country's best rides are on the road. Once we get past these smooth-surfaced pathways, though, adventures in dirt await us.

Rails-to-Trails. Abandoned rail lines are converted into usable public resources for exercising, commuting, or just enjoying nature. Old rails and ties are torn up and a trail, paved or unpaved, is laid along the existing corridor. This completes the cycle from ancient Indian trading routes to railroad corridors and back again to hiking and cycling trails.

Unpaved Roads are typically found in rural areas and are most often public roads. Be careful when exploring, though, not to ride on someone's unpaved private drive.

Forest Roads. These dirt and gravel roads are used primarily as access to forest land and are generally kept in good condition. They are almost always open to public use.

Singletrack can be the most fun on a mountain bike. These trails, with only one track to follow, are often narrow, challenging pathways through the woods. Remember to make sure these trails are open before zipping into the woods. (At the time of this printing, all trails and roads in this guidebook were open to mountain bikes.)

Open Land. Unless there is a marked trail through a field or open space, you should not plan to ride here. Once one person cuts his or her wheels through a field or meadow, many more are sure to follow, causing irreparable damage to the landscape.

TECHNIQUES TO SHARPEN YOUR SKILLS

Many of us see ourselves as pure athletes—blessed with power, strength, and endless endurance. However, it may be those with finesse, balance, agility, and grace that get around most quickly on a mountain bike. Although power, strength, and endurance do have their places in mountain biking, these elements don't necessarily form the framework for a champion mountain biker.

The bike should become an extension of your body. Slight shifts in your hips or knees can have remarkable results. Experienced bike handlers seem to flash down technical descents, dashing over obstacles in a smooth and graceful effort as if pirouetting in Swan

Lake. Here are some tips and techniques to help you connect with your bike and float gracefully over the dirt.

Braking

Using your brakes requires using your head, especially when descending. This doesn't mean using your head as a stopping block, but rather to think intelligently. Use your best judgment in terms of how much or how little to squeeze those brake levers.

The more weight a tire is carrying, the more braking power it has. When you're going downhill, your front wheel carries more weight than the rear. Braking with the front brake will help keep you in control without going into a skid. Be careful, though, not to overdo it with the front brakes and accidentally toss yourself over the handlebars. And don't neglect your rear brake! When descending, shift your weight back over the rear wheel, thus increasing your rear braking power as well. This will balance the power of both brakes and give you maximum control.

Good riders learn just how much of their weight to shift over each wheel and how to apply just enough braking power to each brake, so not to "endo" over the handlebars or skid down a trail.

GOING UPHILL—*Climbing Those Treacherous Hills*

Shift into a low gear (push the shifter away from you). Before shifting, be sure to ease up on your pedaling so there is not too much pressure on the chain. Find the gear best for you that matches the terrain and steepness of each climb.

Stay seated. Standing out of the saddle is often helpful when climbing steep hills with a road bike, but you may find that on dirt, standing may cause your rear tire to lose its grip and spin out. Climbing requires traction. Stay seated as long as you can, and keep the rear tire digging into the ground. Ascending skyward may prove to be much easier in the saddle.

Lean forward. On very steep hills, the front end may feel unweighted and suddenly pop up. Slide forward on the saddle and lean over the handlebars. This will add more weight to the front wheel and should keep you grounded.

Keep pedaling. On rocky climbs, be sure to keep the pressure on, and don't let up on those pedals! The slower you go through rough trail sections, the harder you will work.

GOING DOWNHILL—*The Real Reason We Get Up in the Morning*

Shifting into the big chainring before a bumpy descent will help keep the chain from bouncing off. And should you crash or disengage your leg from the pedal, the chain will cover the teeth of the big ring so they don't bite into your leg.

Relax. Stay loose on the bike, and don't lock your elbows or clench your grip. Your elbows need to bend with the bumps and absorb the shock, while your hands should have a firm but controlled grip on the bars to keep things steady. Steer with your body, allowing your shoulders to guide you through each turn and around each obstacle.

Don't oversteer or lose control. Mountain biking is much like downhill skiing, since you must shift your weight from side to side down narrow, bumpy descents. Your bike will have the tendency to track in the direction you look and follow the slight shifts and leans of your body. You should not think so much about steering, but rather in what direction you wish to go.

Rise above the saddle. When racing down bumpy, technical descents, you should not be sitting on the saddle, but standing on the pedals, allowing your legs and knees to absorb the rocky trail instead of your rear.

Drop your saddle. For steep, technical descents, you may want to drop your saddle three or four inches. This lowers your center of gravity, giving you much more room to bounce around.

Keep your pedals parallel to the ground. The front pedal should be slightly higher so that it doesn't catch on small rocks or logs.

Stay focused. Many descents require your utmost concentration and focus just to reach the bottom. You must notice every groove, every root, every rock, every hole, every bump. You, the bike, and the trail should all become one as you seek singletrack nirvana on your way down the mountain. But if your thoughts wander, however, then so may your bike, and you may instead become one with the trees!

WATCH OUT!
Back-road Obstacles

Logs. When you want to hop a log, throw your body back, yank up on the handlebars, and pedal forward in one swift motion. This clears the front end of the bike. Then quickly scoot forward and pedal the rear wheel up and over. Keep the forward momentum until you've cleared the log, and by all means, don't hit the brakes, or you may do some interesting acrobatic maneuvers!

Rocks and Roots. Worse than highway potholes! Stay relaxed, let your elbows and knees absorb the shock, and always continue applying power to your pedals. Staying seated will keep the rear wheel weighted to prevent slipping, and a light front end will help you to respond quickly to each new obstacle. The slower you go, the more time your tires will have to get caught between the grooves.

Water. Before crossing a stream or puddle, be sure to first check the depth and bottom surface. There may be an unseen hole or large rock hidden under the water that could wash you up if you're not careful. After you're sure all is safe, hit the water at a good speed, pedal steadily, and allow the bike to steer you through. Once you're across, tap the breaks to squeegee the water off the rims.

Leaves. Be careful of wet leaves. These may look pretty, but a trail covered with leaves may cause your wheels to slip out from under you. Leaves are not nearly as unpredictable and dangerous as ice, but they do warrant your attention on a rainy day.

Mud. If you must ride through mud, hit it head on and keep pedaling. You want to part the ooze with your front wheel and get across before it swallows you up. Above all, don't leave the trail to go around the mud. This just widens the path even more and leads to increased trail erosion.

Urban Obstacles

Curbs are fun to jump, but like with logs, be careful.

Curbside Drains are typically not a problem for bikes. Just be careful not to get a wheel caught in the grate.

Dogs make great pets, but seem to have it in for bicyclists. If you think you can't outrun a dog that's chasing you, stop and walk your bike out of its territory. A loud yell to Get! or Go home! often works, as does a sharp squirt from your water bottle right between the eyes.

Cars are tremendously convenient when we're in them, but dodging irate motorists in big automobiles becomes a real hazard when riding a bike. As a cyclist, you must realize most drivers aren't expecting you to be there and often wish you weren't. Stay alert and ride carefully, clearly signaling all of your intentions.

Potholes, like grates and back-road canyons, should be avoided. Just because you're on an all-terrain bicycle doesn't mean you're indestructible. Potholes regularly damage rims, pop tires, and sometimes lift unsuspecting cyclists into a spectacular swan dive over the handlebars.

LAST-MINUTE CHECKOVER

Before a ride, it's a good idea to give your bike a once-over to make sure everything is in working order. Begin by checking the air pressure in your tires before each ride to make sure they are properly inflated. Mountain bikes require about 45 to 55 pounds per square inch of air pressure. If your tires are underinflated, there is greater likelihood that the tubes may get pinched on a bump or rock, causing the tire to flat.

Looking over your bike to make sure everything is secure and in its place is the next step. Go through the following checklist before each ride.

- *Pinch the tires to feel for proper inflation.* They should give just a little on the sides, but feel very hard on the treads. If you have a pressure gauge, use that.
- *Check your brakes.* Squeeze the rear brake and roll your bike forward. The rear tire should skid. Next, squeeze the front brake and roll your bike forward. The rear wheel should lift into the air. If this doesn't happen, then your brakes are too loose. Make sure the brake levers don't touch the handlebars when squeezed with full force.
- *Check all quick releases on your bike.* Make sure they are all securely tightened.
- *Lube up.* If your chain squeaks, apply some lubricant.
- *Check your nuts and bolts.* Check the handlebars, saddle, cranks, and pedals to make sure that each is tight and securely fastened to your bike.
- *Check your wheels.* Spin each wheel to see that they spin through the frame and between brake pads freely.
- *Have you got everything?* Make sure you have your spare tube, tire irons patch kit, frame pump, tools, food, water, and guidebook.

Liability Disclaimer

Neither the publisher, the producer, nor the author of this guide assumes any liability for cyclists traveling along any of the suggested routes in this book. At the time of publication, all routes shown on the following maps were open to bicycles. They were chosen for their safety, aesthetics, and pleasure, and are deemed acceptable and accommodating to bicyclists. Safety upon these routes, however, cannot be guaranteed. Cyclists must assume their own responsibility when riding these routes and understand that with an activity such as mountain bike riding, there may be unforeseen risks and dangers.

HOW TO USE THESE MAPS   Map Descriptions

1 Area Locator Map

This thumbnail relief map at the beginning of each ride shows you where the ride is within the state. The ride area is indicated with a star.

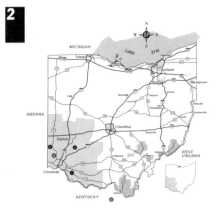

2 Regional Location Map

This map helps you find your way to the start of each ride from the nearest sizeable town or city. Coupled with the detailed directions at the beginning of the cue, this map should visually lead you to where you need to be for each ride.

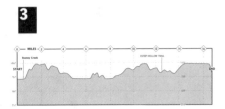

3 Profile Map

This helpful profile gives you a cross-sectional look at the ride's ups and downs. Elevation is labeled on the left, mileage is indicated on the top. Road and trail names are shown along the route with towns and points of interest labeled in bold.

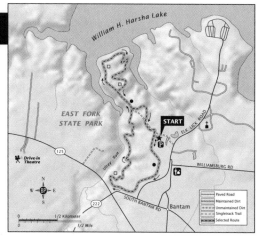

4 Route Map

This is your primary guide to each ride. It shows all of the accessible roads and trails, points of interest, water, towns, landmarks, and geographical features. It also distinguishes trails from roads, and paved roads from unpaved roads. The selected route is highlighted, and directional arrows point the way. Shaded topographic relief in the background gives you an accurate representation of the terrain and landscape in the ride area.

Ride Information (Included in each ride section)

🄲 Trail Contacts:

This is the direct number for the local land managers in charge of all the trails within the selected ride. Use this hotline to call ahead for trail access information, or after your visit if you see problems with trail erosion, damage, or misuse.

🕒 Schedule:

This tells you at what times trails open and close, if on private or park land.

🅢 Fees/Permits:

What money, if any, you may need to carry with you for park entrance fees or tolls.

🄽 Maps:

This is a list of other maps to supplement the maps in this book. They are listed in order from most detailed to most general.

Any other important or useful information will also be listed here such as local attractions, bike shops, nearby accommodations, etc.

We don't want anyone, by any means, to feel restricted to just the roads and trails that are mapped here. We hope you will have an adventurous spirit and use this guide as a platform to dive into Ohio's backcountry and discover new routes for yourself. One of the simplest ways to begin this is to just turn the map upside down and ride the course in reverse. The change in perspective is fantastic and the ride should feel quite different. With this in mind, it will be like getting two distinctly different rides on each map.

For your own purposes, you may wish to copy the directions for the course onto a small sheet to help you while riding, or photocopy the map and cue sheet to take with you. These pages can be folded into a bike bag, stuffed into a jersey pocket, or better still, used with the **BarMap** or **BarMapOTG** (www.cycoactive.com). Just remember to slow or even stop when you want to read the map.

Interstate Highway	
U.S. Highway	
State Road	
County Road	
Township Road	
Forest Road	
Paved Road	
Paved Bike Lane	
Maintained Dirt Road	
Unmaintained Jeep Trail	
Singletrack Trail	
Highlighted Route	
Ntl Forest/County Boundaries	
State Boundaries	
Railroad Tracks	
Power Lines	
Special Trail	
Rivers or Streams	
Water and Lakes	
Marsh	

✝	Airfield	⛳	Golf Course
✈	Airport	🚶	Hiking Trail
🚲	Bike Trail	⛏	Mine
🚳	No Bikes		Overlook
	Boat Launch	🎋	Picnic
)(	Bridge	**P**	Parking
	Bus Stop		Quarry
▲	Campground	((A))	Radio Tower
	Campsite		Rock Climbing
	Canoe Access		School
	Cattle Guard		Shelter
†	Cemetery		Spring
	Church		Swimming
	Covered Bridge		Train Station
	Direction Arrows		Wildlife Refuge
	Downhill Skiing		Vineyard
	Fire Tower	♦♦	Most Difficult
	Forest HQ	♦	Difficult
	4WD Trail	□	Moderate
⌶	Gate	●	Easy

MOUNTAIN BIKE OHIO

The Rides

1. East Fork State Park
2. Ceasar Creek State Park
3. Hueston Woods
4. Alum Creek State Park
5. Paint Creek State Park
6. Scioto Trail
7. Pike State Forest
8. Hanging Rock
9. Pine Creek
10. Bob Evans Farm
11. Survey Marker Trail
12. Snake Hollow ORV Trails
13. Long Ridge
14. Perry State Forest
15. River View
16. Covered Bridge
17. Mickey's Mountain
18. Wellsville
19. Jefferson Lake
20. Beaver Creek State Park
21. Atwood Lake State Park
22. Bear Creek
23. Madison

24. Alpine Valley
25. Vultures Knob
26. Mohican State Park
27. Findley State Park
28. Kelley's Island
29. Maumee State Forest
30. Mary Jane Thurston

Honorable Mentions

A. Harbin Park
B. Big Limestone Trail, KY
C. Deer Creek State Park
D. Richland Furnace
E. Main Corridor
F. Dorr Run
G. Purdum Trail
H. Lake Hope

I. Kanawa State Forest, WV
J. Archer's Fork
K. Lamping Homestead
L. Cuyahoga Valley Towpath
M. Sidecut Metropark
N. Pontiac Lake, MI
O. Potowatami, MI
P. Handlebar Hollow

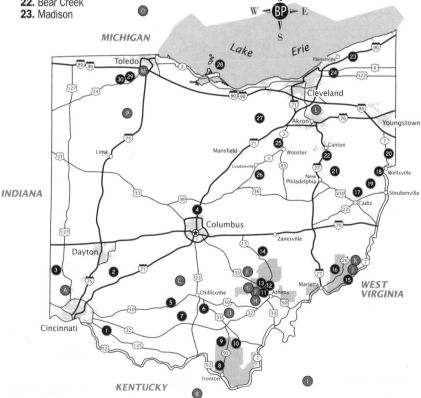

21

COURSES AT A GLANCE Ride Profiles

1. East Fork State Park

Length: 4.4-mile loop
El. Gain: 73 feet
Time: 30 minutes
Difficulty: Easy to Moderate

2. Caesar Creek State Park

Multiple Route Options

Length: 6 miles of trails
El. Gain: Depends on route taken
Time: Rider discretion
Difficulty: Moderate

3. Hueston Woods

Multiple Route Options

Length: 5 miles of trails
El. Gain: Depends on route taken
Time: Rider discretion
Difficulty: Moderate

4. Alum Creek State Park

Multiple Route Options

Length: 5-10 miles
El. Gain: Depends on route taken
Time: Rider discretion
Difficulty: Easy to Moderate

5. Paint Creek State Park

Length: 6.1 miles
El. Gain: 555 feet
Time: 1 hour
Difficulty: Moderate

6. Scioto Trail

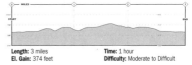

Length: 17.3-mile loop of 30 miles
El. Gain: 1,585 feet
Time: 3 hours
Difficulty: Moderate to Difficult

7. Pike State Forest

Multiple Route Options

Length: Up to 15 miles
El. Gain: Depends on route taken
Time: 2-3 hours
Difficulty: Moderate to Difficult

8. Hanging Rock

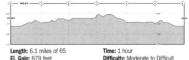

Length: 8.9-mile loop
El. Gain: 720 feet
Time: 1-2 hours
Difficulty: Moderate-Difficult

9. Pine Creek

Length: 12.2-mile out-and-back
El. Gain: 1,113 feet
Time: 1-2 hours
Difficulty: Moderate to Difficult

10. Bob Evans Farm

Length: 3 miles
El. Gain: 374 feet
Time: 1 hour
Difficulty: Moderate to Difficult

11. Survey Marker Trail

Length: 15.4-mile out-and-back
El. Gain: 757 feet
Time: 2 hours
Difficulty: Moderate to Difficult

12. Snake Hollow ORV Trails

Length: 6.1 miles of 65
El. Gain: 679 feet
Time: 1 hour
Difficulty: Moderate to Difficult

13. Long Ridge

Length: 9.1-mile loop of 65 miles
El. Gain: 1,057 feet
Time: 2 hour
Difficulty: Difficult

14. Perry State Forest

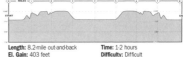
Multiple Route Options

Length: Up to 13 miles
El. Gain: Depends on route taken
Time: Rider discretion
Difficulty: Difficult

15. River View

Length: 11.2-mile out-and-back
El. Gain: 634 feet
Time: 2 hours
Difficulty: Difficult

16. Covered Bridge

Length: 8.2-mile out-and-back
El. Gain: 403 feet
Time: 1-2 hours
Difficulty: Difficult

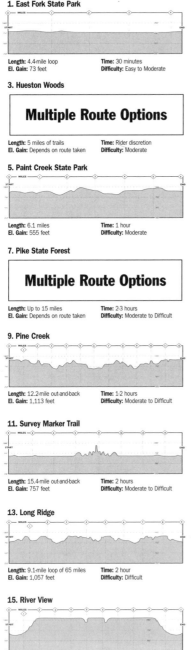

17. Mickey's Mountain

Multiple Route Options

Length: 5 miles per loop
El. Gain: Depends on route taken

Time: 1 hour
Difficulty: Difficult

18. Wellsville

Multiple Route Options

Length: Varies
El. Gain: Depends on route taken

Time: Rider discretion
Difficulty: Difficult

19. Jefferson Lake

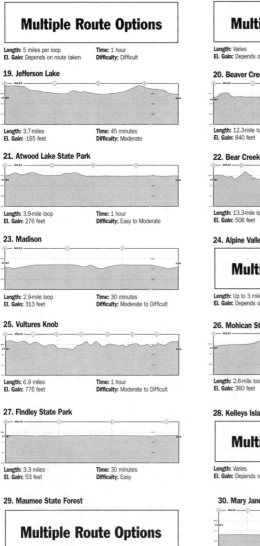

Length: 3.7-miles
El. Gain: -165 feet

Time: 45 minutes
Difficulty: Moderate

20. Beaver Creek State Park

Length: 12.3-mile loop
El. Gain: 840 feet

Time: 2 hours
Difficulty: Moderate to Difficult

21. Atwood Lake State Park

Length: 3.9-mile loop
El. Gain: 276 feet

Time: 1 hour
Difficulty: Easy to Moderate

22. Bear Creek

Length: 13.3-mile loop
El. Gain: 506 feet

Time: 2-3 hours
Difficulty: Difficult

23. Madison

Length: 2.9-mile loop
El. Gain: 313 feet

Time: 30 minutes
Difficulty: Moderate to Difficult

24. Alpine Valley

Multiple Route Options

Length: Up to 3 miles
El. Gain: Depends on route taken

Time: 30-45 minutes
Difficulty: Moderate to Difficult

25. Vultures Knob

Length: 6.9 miles
El. Gain: 776 feet

Time: 1 hour
Difficulty: Moderate to Difficult

26. Mohican State Park

Length: 2.6-mile loop
El. Gain: 360 feet

Time: 30 minutes
Difficulty: Difficult

27. Findley State Park

Length: 3.3 miles
El. Gain: 53 feet

Time: 30 minutes
Difficulty: Easy

28. Kelleys Island

Multiple Route Options

Length: Varies
El. Gain: Depends on route taken

Time: Rider discretion
Difficulty: Easy

29. Maumee State Forest

Multiple Route Options

Length: Up to 5 miles
El. Gain: Depends on route taken

Time: 1 hour
Difficulty: Easy to Moderate

30. Mary Jane Thurston

Length: 6 miles
El. Gain: 74 feet

Time: 1 hour
Difficulty: Easy

1. East Fork State Park
2. Caesar Creek State Park
3. Hueston Woods State Park

Southwest

Honorable Mentions
A. Harbin Park
B. Big Limestone Trail, KY

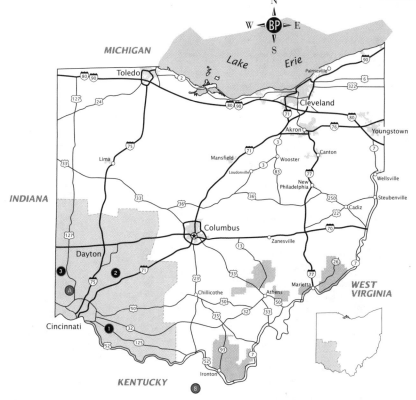

N
W BP E
S

MICHIGAN

Lake Erie

Toledo
Painesville
Cleveland

INDIANA

Lima
Mansfield
Wooster
Canton
Youngstown
Akron
Loudonville
New Philadelphia
Wellsville
Steubenville
Cadiz

Columbus
Zanesville

Dayton

Chillicothe
Athens
Marietta

WEST VIRGINIA

Cincinnati

KENTUCKY

Ironton

Ohio

Southwest Ohio

At the center of this diverse region in Ohio is the city of Cincinnati. Once labeled the Queen City of the West because of how quickly the city grew, Cincinnati is now known for its museums, river front, and, of course, its chili. The city is also home to a large number of people who are all competing for recreation space. Because of this, mountain bikers have been left out of the loop in most urban and suburban areas in southwest Ohio. What opportunities that do exist for riding exist an hour or more from downtown

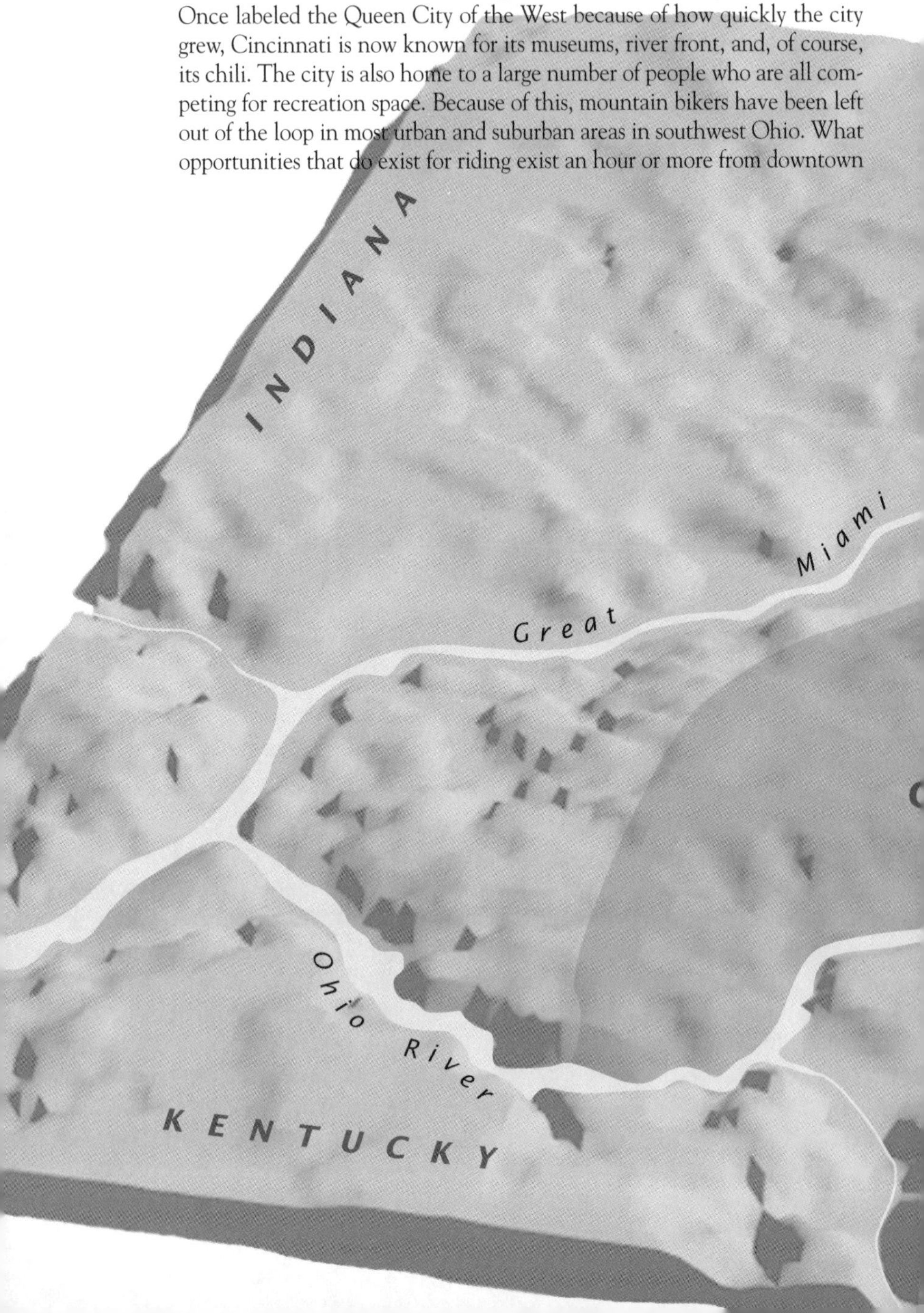

INDIANA

Miami

Great

Ohio River

KENTUCKY

Cincinnati. This situation is not unique to Cincinnati alone. Despite Dayton being the hometown to two of the more famous cyclists in history, Orville and Wilbur Wright, it too has a lack of nearby trail systems.

It is the rolling hills in the countryside, away from the hustle and bustle of city life, where the off-road cyclist can find solace. To the east of Cincinnati is East Fork State Park, which is home to one of the few natural prairies remaining in Ohio. The park provides gentle terrain and excellently maintained trails. To the north of the Queen City is the trail system in Hueston Woods State Park. This maze of trails winds its way near Acton Lake and forests that have been in place since before the War of 1812. Caesar Creek State Park, which is the most heavily used by mountain bikers in the region, hosts a fairly extensive and sometimes confusing trail network. Overuse and lack of a sustained maintenance plan has left trails here damaged and, at times, unusable after a heavy rain.

River

CAESAR CREEK
STATE PARK

Little Miami River

cinnati

East Fork River

East Fork State Park

Ride Summary

Off-road cyclists will encounter few technical obstacles while riding the mountain bike trail at East Fork State Park. Riders probably won't even hit any ruts as the trail is so well maintained. There are a few short hills here at East Fork to keep the thrills high, but overall the trail is relatively easy.

Ride Specs

Start: From the Mountain Bike/World Walker parking lot north of the park office

Length: 4.4-mile loop

Approximate Riding Time: ½ hour

Difficulty Rating: Easy to moderate due to smooth trails and gentle hills

Trail Surface: Singletrack with a few moderate descents and climbs

Lay of the Land: Wooded hills overlooking William Harsha Lake

Elevation Gain: 73 feet

Land Status: State park

Nearest Town: Bethel, OH

Other Trail Users: Hikers

Getting There

From Cincinnati: Take OH 125 east. Turn left on Bantam Road (look for the East Fork State Park entrance). Go left on Park Road #1 past the park office about 0.5 miles to the parking lot access road between two ponds. Park here and ride. **DeLorme: Ohio Atlas & Gazetteer.** Page 75 D-7

E ast Fork State Park probably has one of the best maintained bike trails in the state—a fact not easily overlooked by park visitors. Traveling clockwise from the start, riders will notice that holes have been filled with ash and cinder or simply covered with old shipping pallets, and hills are adequately maintained with rubber waterbars. Riders may be thankful for a hassle-free ride, but they seldom appreciate the work that goes into maintaining a trail like East Fork. Because of its proximity to Cincinnati, the trail receives a lot of traffic. Amazingly, it remains in almost pristine shape. While the riding is often easy, cyclists can appreciate the fact that they seldom come across an overly rutted trail.

The fine folks at the Queen City Wheels cycling club maintain the majority of the trail. Because of its proximity to Kentucky, the Kentucky Mountain Bike Association also lends a hand. These two clubs are well organized and dedicated to the cause of trail access and are a bright spot in

Gentle grades make East Fork a great ride.

a state that suffers from overused and under-maintained trails. If clubs in other parts of the state would follow their lead, there may not be so many trail conflicts in Ohio.

Riding on the trails at East Fork is generally easy, with few sustained climbs, technical descents, or other trail obstacles. The Wisconsin and Illinoian glaciers, leaving much of this area relatively flat, formed much of the terrain you see within the park. Illinoian glacial deposits are rare in

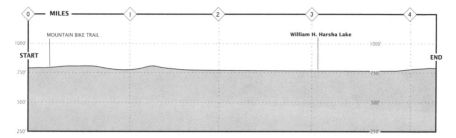

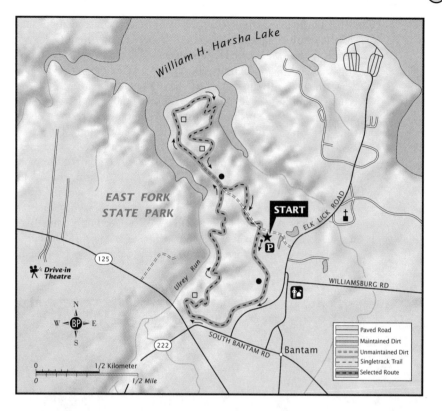

MilesDirections

0.0 START at parking lot by two ponds and about a half-mile north of the park office.

0.1 The mountain bike trail splits; go right.

1.0 The trail goes to other side of ridge.

1.2 The trail follows a gully.

1.4 The mountain bike trail looks over a valley. Stay on top of the ridge.

1.7 The trail follows another gully.

1.9 The mountain bike trail crosses over the hiking trail. Go straight.

2.0 Go left, following the walking trail for a short distance.

2.3 Turn left.

3.1 The mountain bike trail looks over William H. Harsha Lake.

3.8 The trail retraces itself for a little while here.

4.0 Hop back onto the walking trail. Go straight.

4.1 Turn right following the mountain bike trail marker.

4.4 Go straight across the hiking trail and shortly thereafter turn left back to parking lot.

Ohio, but can be found within the park. The glaciers made conditions suitable for the prairies that remain, a rare occurrence in a state that was known by the first settlers who arrived for its impenetrable forests and swamps. At the beginning of the 19th Century, these prairies were home to buffalo and elk. Unfortunately, these roaming herds have long since disappeared due to overhunting and loss of habitat. While the mountain bike trail does not venture onto any of the prairies within the park, it's worth taking a diversion and checking out these habitats that are quite unusual in Ohio.

While there is little trace of the buffalo or elk that once roamed these plains, the ancient Indian cultures that lived alongside them have more clearly left their mark. A mound near Elk Lick Road, built by the Adena and Hopewell tribes, still survives. To this day the mounds and the tribes who built them remain somewhat shrouded in mystery. What historians do know is that the Adena (and later the Hopewell) arrived in the Ohio River basin some 3,000 years ago. The Adena were among the first peoples of the area to subsist primarily on agriculture. No longer did these people have to

Refueling after the ride.

Ride Information

Trail Contacts:
Queen City Wheels
Cincinnati, OH
(513) 677-PELO
www.qcw.org

East Fork State Park
Bethel, OH
(513) 734-4323

Schedule:
Open year-round

❓ Local Information:
Greater Cincinnati Convention & Visitor's Bureau
Cincinnati, OH
1-800-246-2987

➖ Accommodations:
East Fork State Park Camp Office,
Bethel, OH (513) 724-6521

🚹 Organizations:
Queen City Wheels
Cincinnati, OH
(513) 677-PELO
www.qcw.org

The Kentucky Mountain Bike Association
PO Box 5433
Louisville, KY 40255-0433
www.kymba.org

☞ Local Bike Shops:
Bio Wheels
Cincinnati, OH
(513) 861-BIKE
www.biowheels.com

Campus Cyclery
Cincinnati, OH
(513) 721-6628
www.campuscyclery.com

Oakley Cycles
Cincinnati, OH
(513) 731-9111
www.oakleycycles.com

Wright Brothers Cyclery
Montgomery, OH
(513) 489-2222
www.wrightbros.com

Maps:
USGS maps: Batavia, OH; Williamsburg, OH

---

devote every moment to the search for food or shelter. They could settle in one place and devote time to arts, religion, and other activities. The Adena chose to express themselves by building huge mounds, the significance of which still baffles researchers. It is known that the mounds were used, in part, as burial sites. Human remains have been uncovered from within, as have various trinkets and tools. But any clues to the mounds' religious significance (legends and tall tales aside) have yet to be discovered.

Caesar Creek
State Park

Ride Summary

The trails at Caesar Creek are typical of Ohio singletrack riding. They're generally tight and twisty and come with lots of downed logs and roots. Plenty of technical challenges await cyclists in the form of roots and steep ravine crossings. There are relatively few big hills found here, but there are a couple of nice descents to the lake. The trails are not well marked, despite what the park service says.

Ride Specs

Start: From the trailhead near the end of Harveysburg Road
Length: Approximately 6 miles of inter-connected loops
Approximate Riding Time: 1½ hours
Difficulty Rating: Technically moderate due to the steep and often muddy trails
Trail Surface: Singletrack
Lay of the Land: Tight singletrack with steep ravine traverses
Land Status: State park
Nearest Town: Waynesville
Other Trail Users: Hikers

Getting There

From Dayton: Take I-75 south. Turn left (east) onto OH 73. Just after crossing Caesar Creek Lake, turn left on Harveysburg Road. Follow Harveysburg Road past the houses and park at the mountain bike trailhead or a little down the road in the parking area to the left.
DeLorme: Ohio Atlas & Gazetteer: Page 65, D-7; page 66, D-1

ven before the formation of the original 13 American colonies, adventurous souls were making the long journey westward to the Ohio River Valley in search of new farmland, new hunting grounds, and new adventures. French explorers and traders were probably in the region by the late 1600s. With the establishment of trading posts, followed by frontier garrisons, settlers began trickling into Ohio in the early 1700s. In 1774 John Findlay became the first American to reach the Ohio River. The first British traders ventured into the Ohio River Basin that same year.

The journey from the eastern United States to the Ohio River Valley was quite arduous, as the region's muddy soil made all kinds of travel very difficult. Those pulling wagons often found their wheels stuck up to the axles in the thick, clay soil. Still, the mud wasn't enough to keep the settlers from coming and as a result the Native Americans in the area were presented with an even greater challenge: that of defending their territory from the onslaught of white men.

Not all of the men fighting against the settlers were of Indian blood. The most famous white warrior was Blue Jacket, an American kidnapped by the Shawnee as a boy. He eventually became a war chief and one of the fiercest opponents the settlers would face in the conquest of the Northwest Territory. Another lesser-known non-Indian warrior was

It can get pretty thick at Caesar Creek.

Caesar. Formerly a slave to a settler along the Ohio River, Caesar was captured by the Shawnee. He later became one of Blue Jacket's warriors and accompanied him on many raids. He was eventually so well liked by the Shawnee that they gave him an entire valley to use as his personal hunting ground. Little else is known about Caesar, except that Caesar Creek State Park now bears his name.

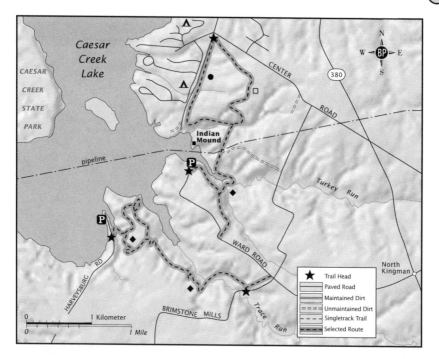

MilesDirections

Because of the crisscross nature of this trail system, it is impossible to recommend a suitable loop for this ride. Just ride, have fun, and remember where you parked.

Today about six miles of trails are open to mountain biking on Caesar's old land. Generally the terrain is rolling, but there are a few short and steep climbs and descents. When it rains the lack of trail maintenance becomes painfully apparent. In many places the trails have been worn down so much by overuse that water collects and forms huge mud holes. It's not uncommon to have your wheels sucked in up to their hubs.

While it is difficult to become hopelessly lost on the park's trails, paths tend to venture off in all different directions. Park maps (good for locating trailheads but little else) say that the trails are marked with four-by-four posts, but most trails are not. Trails simply cut through the woods in random fashion. This web-like network of trails is not necessarily bad, however, as it allows riders to create many different loops.

Ride Information

Trail Contact:
Caesar Creek State Park
Waynesville, OH
(513) 897-3055

Schedule:
Open year-round

Local Information:
Caesar Creek State Park
Waynesville, OH
(513) 897-3055

Accommodations:
Caesar Creek State Park
Waynesville, OH
(513) 897-3055

Maps:
USGS map: New Burlington, OH

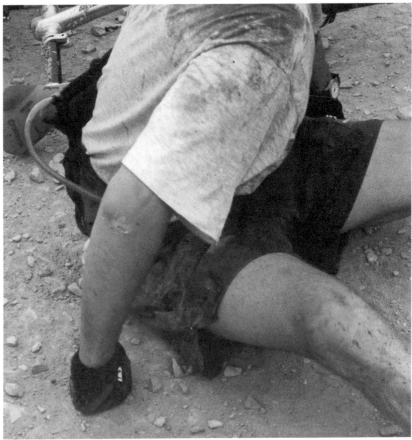

Post crash, pre-bleeding.

Ohio Websites

www.weatherunderground.com
> A nice resource for finding out current and forecast conditions easily. Usually fairly accurate.

www.sitesonline.com
> A comprehensive list of OH sites organized by region. Offers traffic info, limitless links, maps, and other useful information.

http://usparks.miningco.com
> The National Parks homepage has links to each national park and some other interesting info. Also good source if you want to look up historic sites or other points of interest within national parks.

www.nps.gov/daav
> Dayton Aviation Heritage National Park has some interesting links. Of interest to anyone who cares about the Wright brothers or Neil Armstrong, etc.

www.wpafb.af.mil/museum
> US Air Force Museum on Wright-Patterson Air Force Base
> Another aviation site, but looks cool. Says it's the largest military air museum in the world.

www.dnr.state.oh.us/odnr/parks
> Ohio State Parks homepage. It's actually fairly user friendly. A lot of the bike rides in this book are in state parks. Readers can find all sorts of info on each park, including entertainment, accommodations, etc. This one is pretty nice.

www.ohioparks.net
> This is pretty similar to the above state parks address (theme-wise), and it's also a pretty good resource. All Ohio state parks and forests can be found at this site with a description of the area, activities, contacts, and other local attractions.

www.trailmonkey.com/ohhike
> Ohio Hiking Trails and Maps
> Detailed descriptions of trails, areas, maps, and other links.

www.hiayh.org
> Youth hostel information across the nation—helps in planning vacations on a budget, etc.

Hueston Woods

Ride Summary

Hueston Woods State Park is a popular retreat for mountain bikers from Dayton and Cincinnati. While only about five miles of trails within the park are designated for mountain biking, there is plenty of terrain and variety to keep all riders—from beginners to experts—occupied and happy. The climbs are slight, the field riding is wide open, and the downhills and singletrack are fast. Just keep an eye out for abrupt turns that can send you and your bike into the trees.

Ride Specs

Start: From Julie's Mountain Bike Rentals on the north end of the lake
Length: About 5 miles
Approximate Riding Time: 1 hour or more
Difficulty Rating: Technically moderate due to short climbs, sharp turns, and twisty descents
Trail Surface: Singletrack
Lay of the Land: Rolling hills with open fields and tight trails
Land Status: State park
Nearest Town: College Corner
Other Trail Users: Hikers and picnickers

Getting There

From Oxford: Head north on OH 732. After about five miles, turn left at the park entrance. Follow this road to Julie's Mountain Bike Rentals at the north side of the lake. Park there. The trails are right across the road from the store.
DeLorme: Ohio Atlas & Gazetteer. Page 64, D-1

The forests of Hueston Woods State Park, set aside for conservation more than 200 years ago, were probably the first in the state to be deliberately preserved by its white settlers. Today few mountain bikers realize the history behind this National Natural Landmark.

Soon after the conclusion of the Revolutionary War, the leaders of the infant United States of America sought to expand their territories. First on their list was the area known as the Northwest Territory (now called the Midwest). The soil here was fertile, but settlement could not occur until the Native Americans of the area were eliminated or controlled. And that would not be easy: The recently-defeated British still maintained strongholds along the Great Lakes, and from this vantage point were able to incite Native American tribes to resist the American movement.

President George Washington, never one to be dissuaded, sent an expedition led by Colonel Josiah Harmar to fight these belligerent Indian tribes, but the expedition was soundly defeated by the Miami Indians. Later, in 1791, an expedition led by General Arthur St. Clair was even more disastrous—more than 690 men and women, including nearly 40 high-ranking officers, were killed.

The power line has some fun descents.

Still, Washington would not give up, and he sent a third expedition in 1794. General "Mad" Anthony Wayne was appointed to lead the army, and he trained his men for more than two years before heading into battle. In the Battle of Fallen Timbers, Wayne and his troops soundly defeated the Miami Confederation and then moved north to drive the British from the Great Lakes. The Northwest Territory was now open for settlement.

One of General Wayne's soldiers, Matthew Hueston, noticed the fertile soil of the Ohio region and decided to remain there when his campaign with Wayne ended. Hueston purchased land in what are now Butler and Preble Counties, and although he cleared much of the land for cultivation, he left a portion forested. Hueston's descendants also left this wooded land untouched.

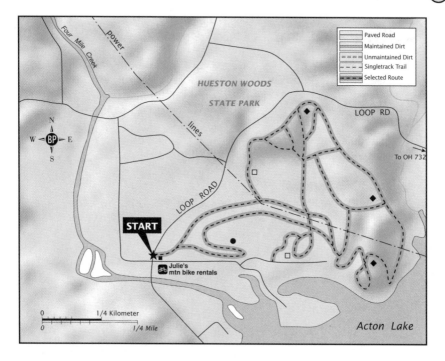

MilesDirections

Because of the nature of the trails in Hueston Woods State Park, a specific route cannot be recommended. Paths crisscross far too often to attempt to follow any particular course. Getting lost is not a problem, though—all the trails loop back to the power line. The trailhead can easily be reached from the far west end of the power line.

Ride Information

● Trail Contact:
Hueston Woods State Park
College Corner, OH
(513) 523-6347

● Schedule:
Open year-round

● Local Information:
Hueston Woods State Park
College Corner, OH
(513) 523-6347

● Accommodations:
Hueston Woods State Park
(camping)
College Corner, OH
1-800-282-7275

● Local Bike Shops:
Julie's Mountain Bike Rentals
Hueston Woods State Park
College Corner, OH

The Bike Center
Oxford, Ohio
1-800-927-0013

● Maps:
USGS map: College Corner, OH

While much of Ohio's original forests have long since vanished, a tract of about 200 acres remains. Through the efforts of conservationists, Hueston Woods, along with other lands bordering the old-growth forest, was designated a state forest in 1941. In 1956 Acton Lake was impounded and the area became a state park. Today there are about five miles of trails in the park open to mountain bikers.

The most obvious feature of the mountain bike trails at Hueston Woods is the power line. Some of the best downhills in the area—long, fast, and full of sweeping curves and dips sure to put a smile on your face—are located on the trails beneath it. Most of the trails are on the north side of the line. These consist of a myriad of twisty tree-lined paths with short, steep climbs and rutted descents. The trails on the south side of the power line are similar to those to the north, only shorter.

Many of the trails offer an excellent view of Acton Lake (pondering life's questions is much easier with a lakefront view). The shore of the lake is prime sunset-watching territory. On days with no wind, the glass-like surface of the water reflects the red and orange hues of the descending sun. In autumn the red and orange leaves of the stately beech and maple trees that line the trails along its shore glow even brighter in the evening light.

It is possible to ride Hueston Woods in a big loop, but the trails crisscross so much that it is best just to go wherever your wheels take you. Faster riders will appreciate the tight singletrack in the woods and the wide-open speed that is possible along the power line, but the trails are easy enough for beginners to try without any fear of getting hurt.

Honorable Mentions

Southwest Ohio

Compiled here is an index of great rides in the Southwest region that didn't make the A-list this time around but deserve recognition. Check them out and let us know what you think. You may decide that one or more of these rides deserves higher status in future editions or, perhaps, you may have a ride of your own that merits some attention.

(A) Harbin Park

Harbin Park, in the city of Fairfield, offers about five miles of trails in mountain-bike-deficient Southwest Ohio. Much of the trail meanders through fields, but there is some singletrack to get your fix. The park hosts a series of races, and the course is marked throughout the year.

From Cincinnati follow Interstate 275 to U.S. Route 127 North. From U.S. Route 127 turn left on Hunter Road, which dead-ends at Harbin Park. For more information call Fairfield Parks and Recreation at (513) 867-5384. *DeLorme: Ohio Atlas & Gazetteer:* Page 74, B-3

(B) Big Limestone Trail, Kentucky

This 18-mile out-and-back follows ridgelines and has some large hills. Near the end of the ride the trail splits—the left line is longer doubletrack and the right is shorter and more technical. They both go the same place.

From Cincinnati take Interstate 75 South to Interstate 64 East in Lexington, Kentucky. Take Interstate 64 to Kentucky 32 (Exit 137), then go south to Morehead, Kentucky. In Morehead turn right (west) onto U.S. Route 60. At Kentucky 519 turn left. Five miles later, turn right at Kentucky 1274. Turn right on Forest Service Road 16, which is gravel. At the fork in the road go right. The trail begins where the road ends. Call (606) 745-3100. *DeLorme: Kentucky Atlas & Gazetteer:* Page 40, E-2

Central

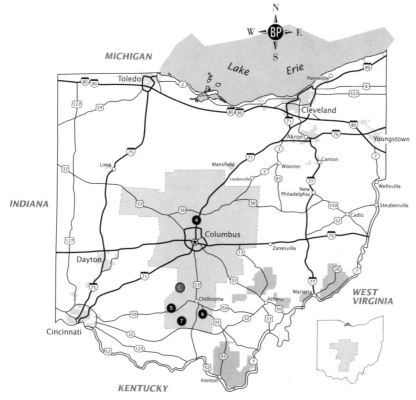

The state capital of Ohio is where you might expect to find it—in the center of the state. Columbus resides on land that more than a million years ago was under ice. As the glaciers retreated, the land was graded smooth. Most of the relief you'll find today exists due to the erosive power of streams.

Although the rail systems in this region are known to get very muddy after a heavy rain, the rides they offer are well worth a little mud in the eye. Alum Creek State Park offers cyclists a fairly long ride that skirts Alum Creek Lake. Scioto Trail state forest and state park offer the most complete and well-marked set of trails in the state. With their long, fast, winding singletrack descents, these trail networks could arguably be the best ride in Ohio. Paint Creek and Pike State Forest are also excellent rides. Paint Creek is a nice mix of easy doubletrack and technical singletrack, while Pike State Forest is a blistering fast ride on wide ORV trails.

With the help of concerned mountain bikers in both Columbus and Chillicothe, the riding opportunities in Central Ohio will only expand. Land managers and park rangers in the region have been very pleased with the results of the mountain bike policies.

Alum Creek State Park

Ride Summary

When it's dry, Alum Creek and its network of trails provide a fun, fast, and twisty ride through the woods of central Ohio. There are no major climbs—a good thing for beginning cyclists—but there are plenty of creek crossings and short and steep hills to challenge experienced riders. The trails wind all over the place so it's possible to ride for hours and never pass the same spot twice.

Ride Specs

Start: From the parking lot on Africa Road

Length: 5–10 miles, depending on which trails you choose

Approximate Riding Time: 30 min.–2 hours, depending on which trails you ride

Difficulty Rating: Moderate due to the twisty nature of the singletrack

Trail Surface: Singletrack

Lay of the Land: Twisty singletrack with a few hills

Land Status: State park

Nearest Town: Delaware

Other Trail Users: Hikers

Getting There

From Delaware: Drive east on U.S. 36. Turn right (south) on Africa Road. Continue for about fve miles and turn left (east) on Lewis Center Road. The parking lot for the mountain biking area is on the left. *DeLorme: Ohio Atlas & Gazetteer.* Page 58, C-2

On a moonless night a small group of refugees stumbles through the wilderness, trying not to make a sound. Their only guides are the waters of Alum Creek and the ghostly white sycamore trees that line its banks. They have left, under the cover of darkness, the nearby Hanby House in Westerville and are slowly making their way to Canada and freedom. The refugees, escaped slaves from the states south of the Ohio River, cannot be discovered or they will be severely punished and returned to their owners.

In the years before the Civil War, Ohio served as one of the primary destinations of escaped slaves on the Underground Railroad. More than 40,000 slaves took many different routes through Ohio as they migrated north.

Expect some mud at Alum Creek

Today Africa Road, along the west end of the mountain bike area of Alum Creek State Park, stands as a reminder of the history of struggle and triumph that took place here more than a century ago.

The modern history of the area began when soldiers from the Revolutionary War settled the newly founded Northwest Territory. Soldiers who fought for their freedom were given land because the American Army could not afford to pay them cash. Later New Englanders, including Quakers and Wesleyan Methodists, settled the fertile Ohio lands. These people, who earlier fled from persecution themselves, aided the escaped slaves through central Ohio.

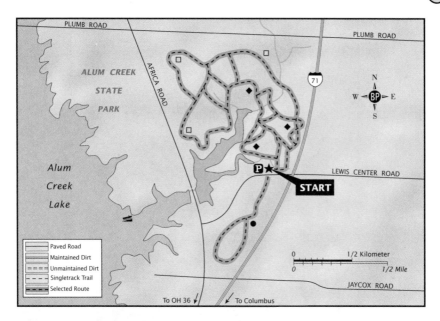

MilesDirections

No specific directions can be given for this ride due to the number of trails and their tendency to crisscross one another. Just ride wherever your bike takes you and enjoy.

Ride Information

❶ Trail Contact:
Central Ohio Mountain Bike Organization
Worthington, OH
(614) 847-4396
www.home.columbus.rr.com/combo

❷ Schedule:
Open year-round

❸ Local Information:
Delaware County Convention and Visitor's Bureau
Delaware, OH
1-888-335-6446

❹ Accommodations:
Alum Creek State Park (camping)
Delaware, OH
(614) 548-4631

Delaware County Convention and Visitor's Bureau
Delaware, OH
1-888-335-6446

❺ Local Bike Shop:
Breakaway Cycling and Fitness
Delaware, OH
(614) 363-3232

❻ Maps:
USGS map: Galena, OH

Today Alum Creek is in the mountain biking history books as being the first state park to open its land to cyclists. In the years since, many other parks in the state have opened their boundaries to bikes, but none have committed to mountain-bike specific trails like Alum Creek.

The Alum Creek Trail began as an Eagle Scout project by local resident Travis Fling and quickly gained the support of local bike shops and the Central Ohio Mountain Bike Association. It was cut in an approximately 650-acre area of the park bordered by Lewis Center Road, Interstate 71, Plumb Road, and the Alum Creek Reservoir.

Sycamore trees are still found in the park, serving not as beacons but as obstacles to be avoided. Most of the original trail traverses woodland, but a bit of field riding is found as well. Riders looking for easy ways to get around the mud pits and other obstacles along the original trail have cut many side trails that crisscross like mazes throughout the area. The damage done to the terrain, through both overuse and misuse when the trail is wet, is painfully apparent. It is best to avoid the trails after rains to save wear on the land and on your bike.

The park, established in 1974 with the creation of the Alum Creek Reservoir, is a popular getaway for Columbus residents, most of whom live just 15 minutes to the south. If you tire yourself out on the bike trails, soak up the rays at Ohio's largest inland beach or rent a boat at one of the nearby marinas. Or, if you're too exhausted to do anything but sleep, pitch your tent at one of the park's 300 or so campsites.

Paint Creek State Park

Ride Summary

Paint Creek State Park is truly friendly to mountain bikers. The park has designated trails ranging from easy doubletrack to technical singletrack so that riders of all levels can be challenged. Bike rentals are available, but the equipment may not be the best quality—bring your own if you can. Beginners will find the hills difficult but the views of the farms and forests in the Paint Creek valley rewarding. Advanced riders can fly on the easy sections but will be challenged by the steep ravine crossings.

Ride Specs

Start: From the mountain bike trailhead on Taylor Road
Length: 6.1 miles
Approximate Riding Time: 1 hour
Difficulty Rating: Moderate due to fast sections and challenging, technical singletrack
Trail Surface: Doubletrack and singletrack
Lay of the Land: Hilly
Elevation Gain: 555 feet
Land Status: State park
Nearest Town: Bainbridge
Other Trail Users: Hikers and hunters

Getting There

From Chillicothe: Head east on U.S. 50. When you get to Rapid Forge Road, turn right. After about three miles turn left on Taylor Road and proceed to the campground. Begin the ride from the camp store. **DeLorme: Ohio Atlas & Gazetteer.** Page 77, C-6

The abrupt hills of the Paint Creek region rise dramatically from the plains at the edge of the Appalachian Plateau. They continue, separated by wide and fertile valleys, until they meet more gentle, rolling hills further to the east, a landscape formed by glaciers whose fingers reached only this far during the last ice age.

It was in the region's valleys that some of the first inhabitants of Ohio settled and left their mark. The earliest known inhabitants were the Adena Mound Builders. Scientists from around the world have yet to determine why the mounds, including Serpent Mound, Adena Mound, and many others, were built by these early Indians.

There is, however, no mystery as to why mountain bikers flock to this area. For riders, the hilly terrain means there are some great descents. The main loop at Paint Creek State Park is all doubletrack, with about equal

The downhill in the field is fast and fun

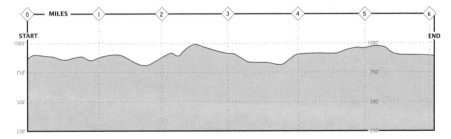

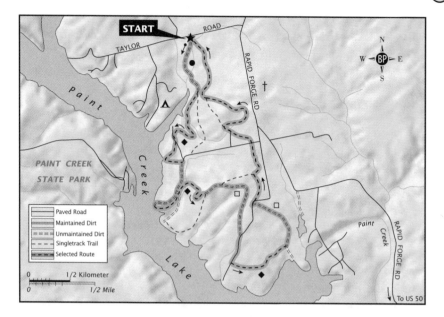

MilesDirections

0.0 START at the mountain bike trail-head on Taylor Road.

0.3 Cross a creek.

0.4 At the top of the hill, take the single-track trail to the right.

0.5 Cross the creek at the bottom of the ravine.

0.8 Cross the ravine then make the diffi-cult descent into another ravine.

0.9 At the main trail turn right.

1.2 Follow the white arrows straight.

1.5 Continue straight past an overgrown trail.

1.7 The mountain bike trail goes left.

1.9 Follow the singletrack trail to the left.

2.0 Cross another ravine.

2.2 After the ravine crossing, the trail zigzags along the ridge.

2.9 Turn left onto the main trail.

3.0 Turn right at the top of the hill.

3.4 Prepare to turn left at the bottom of a fast descent.

3.6 Follow the trail to the left.

3.8 Follow the trail to the right.

4.3 The trail veers right after passing an old house.

4.5 Continue straight past the overgrown trail.

4.9 Continue straight past another over-grown trail.

5.0 After entering the woods, take the singletrack trail to the right.

5.3 Cross a ravine.

5.3 Take the main trail to the right.

6.0 Cross the creek.

59 You are now back on Taylor Road. The camp store is to the left.

Ride Information

🕓 Trail Contacts:
Just North Of Daytona
Chillicothe, OH
(704) 775-SURF

Paint Creek State Park
Bainbridge, OH
(937) 365-1401

🕐 Schedule:
Open year-round, except during hunting season. Contact Paint Creek State Park for various hunting-season schedules.

❓ Local Information:
**Highland County
Chamber of Commerce**
Hillsboro, OH
(937) 393-4883

**Ross/Chillicothe Convention
and Visitors Bureau**
Chillicothe, OH
1-800-413-4118

🔆 Local Attractions:
The Seven Caves, located on U.S. 50 east of Hillsboro, two miles west of Bainbridge. Self-guided caves high on the cliffs (937) 365-1283

⚙ Local Bike Shop:
Just North Of Daytona
Chillicothe, OH
(704) 775-SURF

Ⓝ Maps:
USGS maps: Bainbridge, OH; Greenfield, OH; Rainsboro, OH; South Salem, OH

parts passing through woods and meadows. When park officials built the trails they cleared the routes with a brush hog. While this resulted in trails free of debris and vegetation, it also created some pretty mellow terrain. Beginners, therefore, will find plenty of options. And experts—those who like to push the big chain ring—will find these trails perfect for all-out speed. Still, the singletrack off-shoots from the main trail must be negotiated with caution, no matter how skilled a cyclist you are. If it's wet, some of the steeper singletrack downhills can be very slick. There are a few short technical climbs, but most of the hills are gradual and nothing is too tortuous.

In fact, Paint Creek State Park is very cycling friendly. Park officials have created six miles of trail to suit all levels of mountain bikers. When riders requested more technical trails, officials consulted a nearby shop in Chillicothe called, oddly enough, Just North Of Daytona, for assistance with building singletrack. Today more singletrack is in the works. Races, including a 12-hour endurance competition, are held regularly at the park as part of the Kenda Off-Road series. The park also has some of the best camping facilities available in Ohio—a welcome relief after a long day on the saddle.

Scioto Trail State Forest/State Park

Ride Summary

Scioto Trail State Forest is home to one of the longest singletrack trails in the state. But length is not the only asset of this ride. You'll also find challenging climbs and long, fast, and very fun descents. The trail is frequented by all walks of life—from hikers to equestrians—so watch your speed and be ready to step aside. Still, most of the people you come across will be just like you—trail-hungry bikers. **One final note:** The trail can become very muddy when it rains.

Ride Specs

Start: Behind the park office on the corner of Stoney Creek and Lake Roads
Length: 17.3-mile loop of 30-mile trail system
Approximate Riding Time: 3 hours
Difficulty Rating: Moderate to challenging due to steep climbs and bumpy descents
Trail Surface: Singletrack, paved roads, and gravel roads
Lay of the Land: Multiple-use trails on steep, rocky hills with some gravel- and paved-road riding
Elevation Gain: 1,585 feet
Land Status: State forest, state park
Nearest Town: Chillicothe
Other Trail Users: Horseback riders, hikers, and hunters

Getting There

From Chillicothe: Take U.S. 23 south for about 10 miles to the Scioto Trail State Park entrance at OH 372. Turn left on OH 372, then left again onto Lake Road. Park at the park office or farther down the road at the campground amphitheater. *DeLorme: Ohio Atlas & Gazetteer.* Page 78, C-2

Scioto Trail State Forest and Scioto Trail State Park provide Chillicothe-area mountain bikers with some of the finest trails in the state. Thanks to the enthusiasm of the Forest Service, which has done everything it can to balance the needs of riders with those of hikers, horseback riders, and others, miles and miles of new and existing trails are now open to cyclists. One of the newest trails, known simply as the Airport Trail, circles an old airport and is tighter and more technical than some of the area's original trails. It also happens to be quite rocky with some short climbs and descents.

The forest and state park are named for the Scioto Trail, a wide path that once paralleled the Scioto River to its mouth at the Ohio. The trail was used by the region's Native Americans to link the settlement of Chalagawtha (at the junction of Paint Creek and the Scioto River in present day Chillicothe) to the hunting grounds of Kan-tuck-kee on the other side of the Ohio River. There, in a land of rolling hills and pristine meadows, tribes found their fill of elk, buffalo, waterfowl, turkey, and other game. Soon after the arrival of the Europeans, however, the hunting grounds in Kan-tuck-kee lost much of their bounty. Buffalo and elk were slaughtered

MilesDirections

0.0 START at marker 1, behind the forest service maintenance facility on the corner of Stoney Creek and Lake Roads.

0.4 Cross the creek.

0.6 The trail turns left then climbs straight up a hill.

0.8 At the top of the ridge, at marker 2, go left.

1.0 Continue straight. Do not take Buckeye Trail to the right.

1.1 After a grueling climb, relax and enjoy the view to the left.

1.2 Turn left onto the gravel at North Ridge Road.

2.4 At marker 13, turn right onto Long Branch Trail.

3.1 Follow the trail to the right, designated by white trail markers.

3.7 Continue following Long Branch Trail to the right at marker 11. The trail on the left goes to Moss and Toad Hollows.

5.9 Go straight at marker 6. Do not take Cemetery Trail on the right.

6.2 Ride across the gravel parking lot at marker 10. At Stoney Creek Road turn left. Go down the road about 50 yards then take a right at marker 37.

6.8 Turn left at marker 36.

6.9 Cross Airport/Bethel Road to Airport Trail at marker 39.

7.0 Continue straight. Do not take the trail to the left.

7.1 Turn left into the woods and up a short, steep climb.

8.2 Cross the creek then continue along the trail as it parallels the creek.

8.5 Cross another creek then pedal straight across a field.

8.6 Follow the gravel FS 5 to the right.

9.5 Continue on FS 5, ignoring the trail marked "C-9." The bottom of this trail is often wet and the climb out is heinous.

11.6 Take a right on Estep Hollow Trail.

12.2 Go left at marker 34. The old Estep Hollow Trail is off to the right but isn't nearly as fun as the new Estep Hollow Trail.

12.3 Turn left at marker 33.

12.9 Turn left at marker 31.

13.0 Cross the gravel road to marker 44.

13.7 Cross the creek to marker 45, then go right.

13.8 Cross the creek, then go left on Stoney Creek Road (OH 372).

15.3 Pass the fire tower then take a right on Lake Road.

15.4 Pass the carpentry shop.

16.0 Turn right on the Fire Tower Trail to the state park.

16.5 Go right at the fork. The trail to the left simply loops back.

16.6 Go left at the fork. The right trail loops back.

16.7 Go right and descend the very steep hill to the campground.

17.3 Finish at Caldwell Lake Campground. Pedal three-quarters of a mile or so back to the start behind the forest service maintenance facility.

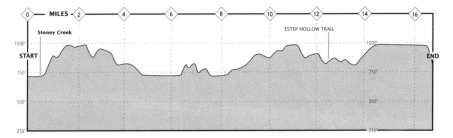

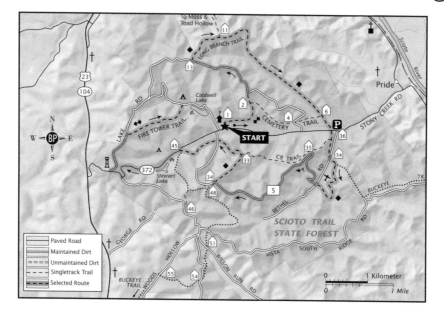

Ride Information

Trail Contacts:
Scioto Trail State Forest
Chillicothe, OH
(740) 663-2523

Scioto Trail State Park
Chillicothe, OH
(740) 663-2125

Schedule:
Open year-round

Local Information:
Ross/Chillicothe Convention and Visitors Bureau
Chillicothe, OH
1-800-413-4118

Local Event/Attraction:
Scioto Trail Mountain Bike Weekend
Scioto Trail State Forest
Chillicothe, OH
(704) 775-SURF

Local Bike Shop:
Just North of Daytona
Chillicothe, OH
(704) 775-SURF

Maps:
USGS map: Waverly North, OH

by the hundreds, often just for their livers, tongues, or hides. The buffalo, elk, and turkey that weren't killed by the shemanese, as the natives called the newcomers, were driven out by the horses and cattle that grazed and depleted the meadows and plains. Wild herds became rare and small, making hunting more difficult for the tribes. While the centuries-old trail does not exist today, drivers can approximate its route—and the sad history it represents—by cruising down U.S. Route 23.

Today locals mostly frequent the forest and, like the Native Americans before them, seem to have a sense of connection with the land. Still, it's unlikely that you'll come across many other users. You may have to contend with an occasional horse-hoof crater, but the forest is so large and contains so many trails that it's rare to see equestrians. And hikers tend to stick to the trails within Scioto Trail State Park (the state forest surrounds the park). Several trails from the state forest lead into the park and make for nice descents at the end of a ride (and, going in the opposite direction, lousy, hike-a-bike ascents).

If you do come across a local, there's a good chance they'll be happy to tell you where the top trails are and where you can find the best views. And speaking of views, be sure to bring a camera. Unlike in most parts of Ohio, vistas of the surrounding hills and valleys are grand and numerous. The best views are found at the beginning of the ride just before North Ridge Road and during the climb up Forest Road 5. The fire tower, when open, also offers an excellent perch from which to scan the surrounding countryside. Fall foliage can be spectacular, too.

But excellent views aren't the only thing Scioto Trail State Forest is famous for. When you're not gazing into the sky and dreaming about distant lands, you'll find yourself tackling one of the longest descents in the state. The trip down the wide (downhill-friendly) Long Branch Trail is almost two miles in length. The Estep Hollow descent isn't quite as long, but it does have plenty of twists and turns to keep things interesting.

Doug on one of the longest descents in Ohio

Pike State Forest

Ride Summary

When it comes to mountain biking, this is probably one of the best ORV areas in Ohio. The trails in Pike State Forest are well marked, well maintained, and, unlike those in most other ORV areas, well designed: They switchback up the hills rather than go straight up and down. The hills are big, permitting challenging climbs and fast descents. There are lots of jumps, too. As there are several loops here, it's easy to spend an entire day and not ride the same route twice.

Ride Specs

Start: ORV trailhead on OH 124
Length: 15 miles
Approximate Riding Time: 2–3 hours
Difficulty Rating: Moderate to difficult due to several water bar crossings and big hill climbs
Trail Type: ORV doubletrack
Terrain: Hilly and wooded
Elevation Gain: 925 feet
Land Status: State forest
Nearest Town: Waverly
Other Trail Users: ORVs and hunters

Getting There

From Columbus: Take U.S. 23 south to Waverly and turn right (west) on OH 220. After about 10 miles, turn right on OH 124. The Pike State Forest ORV trailhead is on the right side of OH 124, about two miles after Bell Hollow Road. *DeLorme: Ohio Atlas & Gazetteer.* Page 77, D-6

O f all the state forests in Ohio, Pike State Forest is probably the most mountain-biker friendly. Park officials and ORV riders alike are happy to see pedal-powered riders. They are amazed that anyone could—or would want to—climb the big hills. ORV riders are even more amazed when mountain bikers keep up with them on the downhills.

Pike State Forest is also better maintained than other ORV areas. An abundance of water bars has kept the trails relatively free of the big ruts that are common on ORV paths in other parts of the state. Many of the water bars are six-inch strips of old tire that stick out of the ground to divert water from flowing straight down the trail. While they can be a bit disconcerting at first, the rubber water bars simply bend out of the way when hit by a fast-moving bike tire.

The other type of water bar you'll encounter looks like a fun jump. On fast descents, however, watch out. If you hit one at a considerable speed it will launch your rear wheel skyward and may cause you to crash. A good

Tree roots are a technical tasty treat

way to clear such a water bar is by using the "speed jump," a technique often employed by BMX racers. To speed jump, first lift your front wheel over the jump; then lift your back wheel to the top of the jump and simply ride off its backside. It's a difficult technique to learn—you might be better off just getting behind your saddle and letting your body absorb the shock of the bump.

While the hills in Pike State Forest are large by Ohio standards—up to 1,200 feet—the climbs and descents are not straight up-and-down affairs. They are by no means gentle, but if you're in decent shape you should be able to conquer them without too much trouble. And with elevation changes of more than 450 feet in places, there are some very long and fast downhills. Screaming through banked turns provides an interesting sensation as you feel the force of gravity pulling you—and your bike—toward the ground. All of the trails here are well marked with numbers (1–19). These numbers do not indicate mileage since there are only 15 miles of trails. However, because there are several loops, it's easy to create a longer ride.

The mud here can become thick after heavy rains, but in general the trails drain fairly well—especially for ORV paths in the southern part of the state. Credit good trail construction for that. When the trails are dry they can be very dusty, so if you're riding with a group of people, make sure you lead the pack on the downhills.

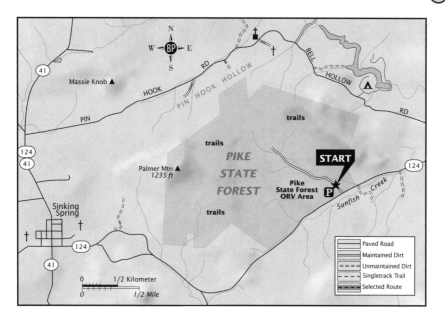

MilesDirections

No specific directions can be given for this ride due to the number of trails and their tendency to crisscross one another. Just ride wherever your bike takes you and enjoy.

Ride Information

🕿 Trail Contact:
Pike State Forest
Latham, OH
(740) 493-2441

🕐 Schedule:
Closed December 1 to March 31

❓ Local Information:
Ross/Chillicothe Convention and Visitors Bureau
Chillicothe, OH
1-800-413-4118

🛏 Accommodations:
Pike Lake State Park (camping)
Bainbridge, OH
(740) 493-1401

🚲 Local Bike Shop:
Just North of Daytona
Chillicothe, OH
(740) 775-SURF

🚩 Maps:
USGS maps: Byington, OH; Sinking Springs, OH

Mountain Biking With Your Dog

Many people love to bring their canine companion along on mountain bike trails. Our furry friends make great trail partners because they're always good company and they never complain. If you take your dog mountain biking with you, or you're considering it, remember that there are a number of important items to keep in mind before hitting the trails.

Getting in Shape

It would be no better for your dog than it would you to tackle running a marathon without first getting into good physical condition. And if your pet has been a foot warmer much of his life, you will need to train him into reasonable shape before taking him along on those long weekend bike rides.

You can start your dog's training regimen by running or walking him around the neighborhood or, better yet, a local park. Frisbees and balls are also great tools to help get your dog physically fit for those upcoming mountain bike rides. Always remember that on a trail your dog probably runs twice as far as you ride. Build your dog's exercise regimen based on the mileage you plan to ride each time you head out. If you're going on a five-mile trail, assume your dog needs to be in shape for a 10-mile trail. Gradually build up your dog's stamina over a two to three month period before committing him to arduous afternoons of trying to keep up with you as you pedal along on your bike.

Training

Teaching your dog simple commands of obedience may help keep both you and your dog out of a heap of trouble while out there on public trails. The most important lesson is to train your dog to come when called. This will ensure he doesn't stray too far from the trail and possibly get lost. It may also protect him from troublesome situations, such as other trail users or perhaps coming in contact with local wildlife. Also teach your dog the "get behind" command. This comes in especially handy when you're on a singletrack trail and you run into other bikers. Teaching your dog to stay behind you and your bike and to follow your lead until the trail is clear can be a valuable and important lesson. Remember also to always carry a long leash with you in case, after all your prior training, you still have to tie your dog up to a tree at a campsite or succumb to local leash laws on crowded trails.

There are a number of good dog training books on the market that should help train you and your dog how to stay out of trouble with other trail users. Also, look to your local SPCA or kennel club for qualified dog trainers in the area.

Nutrition

Nutrition is important for all dogs. Never exercise a dog right after eating for the same reasons people shouldn't exercise right after eating. Feed your pet a high quality diet such as Hills Science Diet™ or Iams™. These products have higher quality ingredients and are more nutritionally balanced than generic grocery store dog foods. They may be more expensive than some generic brands, but your dog also doesn't need to eat as much of it to get the same nutrition and calories. If you insist on feeding your dog a grocery store diet, stick with the Purina™ brand, as it is still better for your dog than most others in this class.

Trail Tips

Try to pick your riding trails near lakes or streams. The biggest threat to your dog when biking is the heat, and water is essential to keep him cool. If the trail doesn't have water nearby then you need to bring as much liquid for him as you would drink yourself. A small lightweight plastic bowl can be used to give your dog water, or you can purchase a collapsible water bowl made from waterproof nylon (Call Ruff Wear™ ; (541) 388-1821). Also, you can use a waterbottle to squirt water into your dog's mouth.

- Try not to take your dog riding with you on a really hot day—hotter than 80 degrees. To avoid these temperatures, take your dog riding in the early morning or evening when the air is cooler and safer for your pet.
- Watch for signs of heat stroke. Dogs with heat stroke will: pant excessively, lie down and refuse to get up, become lethargic and disoriented. If your dog shows any of these signs, immediately hose him down with cool water and let him rest. If you're on the trail and nowhere near a hose, find a cool stream and lay your dog in the water to help bring his body temperature back to normal.
- Avoid the common foot pad injuries. Don't run your dog on hot pavement or along long stretches of gravel road. Always bring a first aid kit that includes disinfectant, cotton wrap, and stretchy foot bandage tape so you can treat and wrap your dog's paw if it becomes injured. You might also want to look into purchasing dog booties, useful for protecting your dog's pads and feet during long runs outdoors.
- Be sure to keep your dog's nails trimmed. If your dog's nails are too long, they might catch on an object along the trail and lead to soft tissue or joint injuries.
- Don't take your dog on crowded trails and always carry a leash with you. Remember, just because you love your dog doesn't mean other people will.

Honorable Mentions

Central Ohio

Noted below is one of the great rides in Central Ohio that didn't make the A-list this time around but deserves recognition nonetheless. Check it out and let us know what you think. You may decide that it deserves higher status in future editions or, perhaps, you may have a ride of your own that merits some attention.

(C) Deer Creek State Park

Deer Creek State Park has 1.2 miles of trails open to mountain bikers through woodlands and fields. Bird watchers may want to visit Deer Creek now that the Ohio Division of Wildlife is re-introducing ospreys to the park. The birds, which are similar to eagles, have been extinct from Ohio since 1913. Up to 20 breeding pairs could be introduced by the end of 2000.

From Columbus, take Interstate 71 South to U.S. Route 62 South. Follow U.S. Route 62 to Mt. Sterling and Ohio 207. Turn left on Ohio 207 (south) then left again on Crownover Mill Road. Take the first left toward the beach. Pass the beach and the trailhead is at the end of the road. For more information call Deer Creek State Park at (740) 869-3124. *DeLorme: Ohio Atlas & Gazetteer:* Page 67, D-7

Southeast

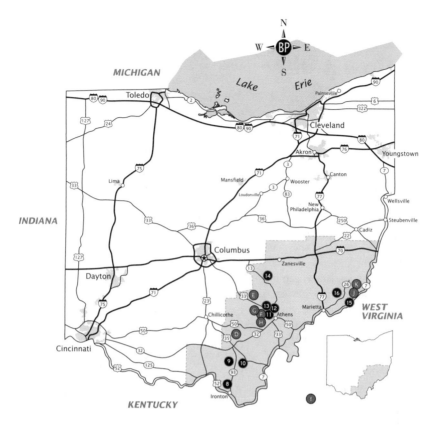

Ohio

Southeast Ohio

As you travel from north to south toward Southeastern Ohio, look for the abrupt change in topography. The relative flatness of the glaciated portion of Ohio meets the undulating landscape of the unglaciated region. Wooded hilltops and deep stream valleys replace the rows of corn common to most areas of Ohio. Southeast Ohio is sometimes referred to as the Gateway to West Virginia. The people of the region don't find that label too appealing, but it does aptly describe the geography of this corner of the state.

The mining industry, which was once the economic mainstay of this region, has since been in decline. The region lacks the infrastructure needed to encourage new industry to settle in the area. But Southeastern Ohio is not without its riches. The wooded land here is rugged and beautiful, and picturesque rivers flow lazily, forming steep hillsides. The Hocking Hills region exemplifies Southeastern Ohio with its sandstone cliffs and deep river valleys. Autumn rides are rewarded with extravagant shades of red, yellow, and orange. Even driving the winding and rolling roads here is worthwhile.

The riding in this region is both challenging and fun. Several of the trails follow wide off-road vehicle (ORV) trails. Though these trails are very fast, they are by no means easy as they are filled with steep climbs and blazing descents. Other trails are primarily challenging singletrack with steep switchbacks and challenging descents.

One common characteristic to all of these trail systems is the clay soil. In the drier summer months the clay of the ORV trails turns to dust and makes life—and visibility—miserable for any rider stuck at the back of the pack. The clay can also be as hard as cement in places. During the rainy season, the clay turns into an evil monster. Clay mud sticks to every part of the bike, wearing out bikes parts in short order. Sometimes there is so much mud that it clogs the wheels and makes it impossible to make any forward progress. But it is a helluva lot of fun.

Determining when it will be wet or dry is not an easy matter. The weather in Southeastern Ohio is often influenced by several weather systems, which makes predicting when it will rain very difficult.

While rehydrating after cranking up and down ridges and valleys of Southeastern Ohio, take a side trip off the saddle to Hocking Hills State Park. The park's six regions total 2,000 acres of pristine forest-covered hillsides and cascading streams. The Hocking Hills region, which is carved out of 350 million year old Black Hand sandstone, is home to several unique geological features, including Ash Cave, Old Man's Cave, and Cedar Falls. The ancient Adena Indians inhabited these caves over 7,000 years ago.

Directions:

From Columbus: Take U.S. 33 east to Logan, OH. From Logan, take OH 93 south to OH 664. Follow the signs and OH 664 to Hocking Hills State Park.

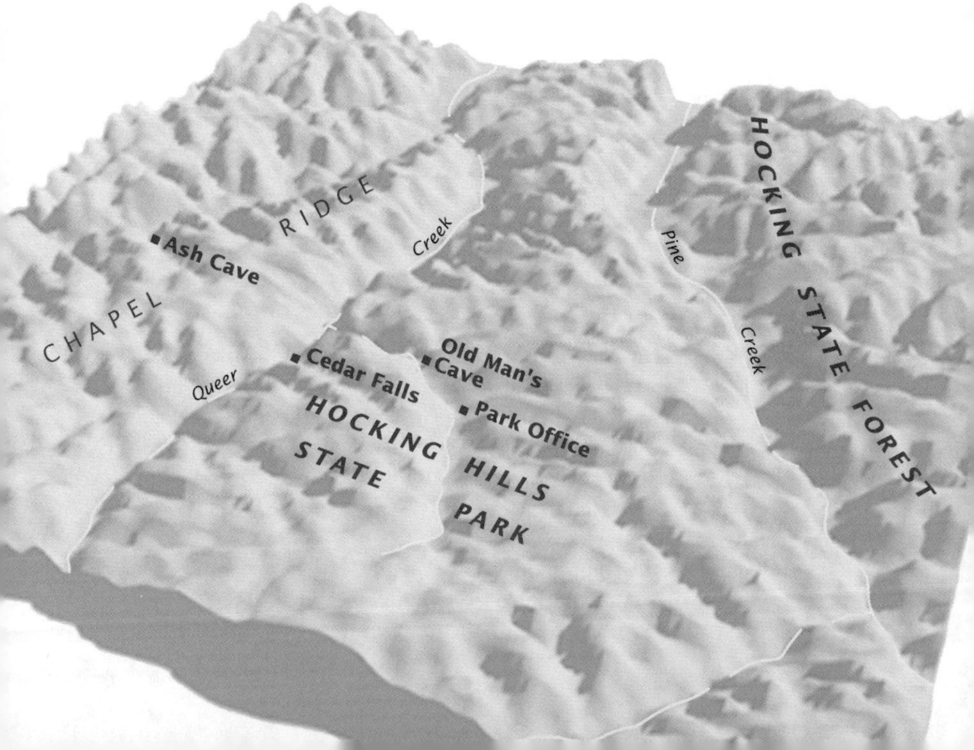

Hanging Rock

Ride Summary

The Hanging Rock trails are more conducive to trail riding than those at Pine Creek because of the many interconnected loops and better facilities. There are about 26 miles of trails here but the length of the ride can vary in many different ways. With so many loops, riders can become confused, but all the intersections are well marked so pinpointing a location on the map is not too difficult. One must-ride trail is Lakeview. As the name implies, this trail offers views of the many lakes and ponds in the forest. Even without the views however, the trail is an exciting ride with high-speed downhills and blazing turns through a beautiful pine forest. If you like to fish, bring a rod—the Forest Service has marked nearly 30 of the best fishing holes.

Ride Specs

Start: Hanging Rock parking area off FS 105

Length: 8.9-mile loop

Approximate Riding Time: 1½ hours

Difficulty Rating: Moderate to difficult due to steep, demanding climbs and rocky descents

Trail Types: Doubletrack and gravel roads

Terrain: Hilly with some rocks and gravel

Elevation Gain: 820 feet

Land Status: National forest

Nearest Town: Ironton

Other Trial Users: ORVs, hunters, and anglers

Getting There

From Ironton: Take OH 52 west approximately four miles to OH 650. Turn left. Follow OH 650 for about one mile and turn left at FS 105. The parking area is at the top of the hill, about one mile up FS 105. *DeLorme: Ohio Atlas & Gazetteer.* Page 85, D-7

T he Native Americans who settled the Ohio River Valley saw this land of hills and forests as a bountiful gift from Moneto, a land full of game and lush with fertile soil. Many European settlers who followed them, however, saw the Native Americans and their land as things to be controlled and conquered. The native tribes were subdued, the wild animals slaughtered, and the forests cleared.

Even with the wanton destruction by the settlers, the forests remained mostly pristine until the introduction of commercial lumbering in 1800. These hardwood forests, among the finest in the world, would not see the

Take some time to explore Hanging Rock's extensive trail system.

next century. At the peak of the Ohio lumber industry in 1849, the state was fourth in the nation in terms of lumber production. First cut were the marketable trees—black walnut, black cherry, and white oak. The remaining trees were removed during later cuts, leaving only undesirable, sick, or defective trees. By 1920 all of the marketable trees were gone and virtually no area in the state had been left uncut. The remaining lands sold for less than $1 per acre.

The Scotch-Irish settlers often burned what forested areas remained. This practice was widely accepted in their native lands where the heath was regularly burned to kill the brush that competed with crops. It also rid the land of snakes, ticks, and other "undesirable" vermin and was thought to eliminate the fever germs that lurked in the forest. The newly cleared land became excellent grazing land for the cattle; only the hardiest trees, such as oak and hickory, could survive.

Riding through the Hanging Rock area's wide ORV trails, the only trees evident are the surviving oak and hickory and the newly planted, quick-growing pines. The soil varies considerably as the trails pass beneath the different types of trees. It is most noticeable in the fall when the slippery oak leaves cover the hard-packed trail while the soil in the pine stands is soft with fallen needles.

MilesDirections

0.0 START from the parking area at the top of the hill. Turn left and head down the road.

0.1 Turn right onto the Hanging Rock Trail.

0.5 Cross the gravel road.

0.7 Turn right at the bottom of the hill.

0.8 Follow the main trail straight.

2.2 Turn right at the bottom of the hill, just above Rock Hollow Road.

2.6 Cross the bridge.

3.4 Turn left (follow the trail markers).

4.4 Cross a bridge.

4.5 Cross another bridge.

4.8 Take the trail to the left and climb steeply up from the creek.

5.2 Enter a grove of pine trees.

5.4 Go right at the edge of the stand of pines.

5.5 Stay right on the main trail (follow the trail markers) and pass marker #6.

5.7 Turn left (follow the Hanging Rock Trail marker). The Lakeview Trail is to the right.

6.0 Continue on the Hanging Rock Trail to the right.

6.7 Follow the trail straight into the pine trees.

7.1 Go straight (follow the main trail markers).

7.2 Take the Sawmill Trail to the right.

7.8 After crossing the road, go right on the Hanging Rock Trail.

7.9 The trail turns right around a lake.

7.9 Turn right onto the Lakeview Trail.

8.1 Go left on the gravel road.

8.9 End the ride at the parking area.

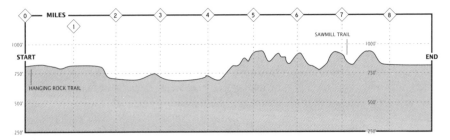

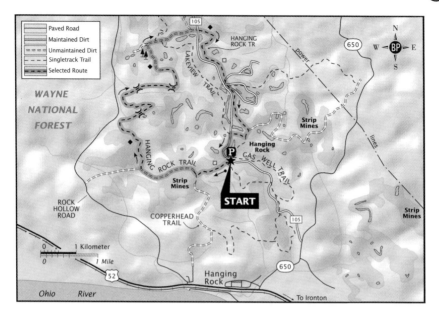

Ride Information

Trail Contact:
Wayne National Forest
Ironton Ranger District
Pedro, OH
(614) 532-3223

Schedule:
April 15 to November 15

Fees/Permits:
The Wayne National Forest is a fee area. Trail passes can be purchased for $5 at Forest Service headquarters in Pedro.

Local Information:
Portsmouth Convention and Visitors Bureau
Portsmouth, OH
(740) 353-1116

Accommodations:
Vesuvius Recreation Area
(primitive camping)
Wayne National Forest
Ironton Ranger District
Pedro, OH
(614) 532-3223

Maps:
USGS map: Ironton, OH

While the region is hilly, there are not as many long climbs at Hanging Rock as in other areas of the Wayne National Forest. The one major climb of the ride comes early on. The rest of the trail consists of a series of more gradual ups and downs, and higher-than-average speeds are easy to maintain.

It's worth spending a couple of days at Hanging Rock. The trail system is extensive and it often takes a couple of rides to become familiar with the layout. But once you've got a handle on the area, you should be able to fly over the rolling trails to the north or blast down the steeper downhills of Hanging Rock's southern section. There's a little bit of everything here for those who have time to explore.

The best trail in the area is the Lakeview Trail. It's a wide roller-coaster ride that twists through a myriad of lakes leftover from the region's mining era. The trail rises and descends 30 to 50 feet over and over again, sending riders up and down and up and down at thrilling speeds.

Coal and iron mining began here in the early 1800s. By 1875 the Hanging Rock Iron District had 69 charcoal furnaces, each of which depended on the surrounding forests for the charcoal required to smelt iron ore. At that time the region was the leading producer of iron ore in the nation. There are still mining and timber operations in the Ironton District of the Wayne National Forest, but much of the land has been restored. The hills are now known for their rugged beauty attracting tourists, campers, and ORV riders who flock to these woods to experience the best of southern Ohio.

Wayne National Forest allows primitive camping on all of its lands, but there are few suitable spots at Pine Creek and Hanging Rock. You'll have better luck finding a site at the Vesuvius Recreation Area, located just south of Pedro. Sites cost $10 a night. Unfortunately, biking is not allowed on the trails in the recreation area. However, just up the road from Vesuvius on Ohio Route 93 is the Forest Service office where you can find maps of all the trails and the required permits.

Pine Creek

Ride Summary

While the Pine Creek trails are similar to trails in the Athens District of the Wayne National Forest, they do differ in several regards: Mainly, there are fewer long climbs, fewer descents, and fewer water bars. Because of this, it's easy to maintain a consistent speed. In fact, if you're looking for all-out velocity, you'll find it here. The ride described below must be done as an out-and-back unless a car is dropped at one of the other trailheads. But don't ride between trailheads unless you're truly hardcore.

Ride Specs

Start: Telegraph Trailhead on Telegraph Hill Road
Length: 12.2-mile out-and-back
Approximate Riding Time: 1½ hours
Difficulty Rating: Technically moderate due to challenging climbs
Physical Difficulty: Physically difficult due to long climbs
Trail Surface: ORV doubletrack
Lay of the Land: Hilly
Elevation Gain: 1,113 feet
Land Status: National forest
Nearest Town: , OH
Other Trail Users: ORVs and hunters

Getting There

From Ironton: Head north on OH 93 for approximately 23 miles to Telegraph Hill Road (CR 193) and the sign for Telegraph Trailhead. Turn left. The trailhead is on the left side of the road, about a quarter of a mile from the OH 93/Telegraph Hill Road intersection. *DeLorme: Ohio Atlas & Gazetteer.* Page 85, B-7

T hanks to the country's appetite for iron ore, the Pine Creek trails of the Wayne National Forest experienced much of the same general degradation as other trail systems in the region.

When the first Welsh settlers arrived in southern Ohio in the early 19th century, they brought with them a wealth of mining experience. Many had mined coal from the hills of Wales, which were very similar to the hills of Ohio.

The areas that now include Jackson, Lawrence, Scioto, and Vinton Counties were abundant in the resources needed to make iron: limestone, iron ore, coal, and wood. With rudimentary tools such as shovels and pick-axes, the miners dug shallow pits and extracted the iron ore. To make charcoal they stacked wood then covered it with damp leaves and soil. When lit, the wood would smolder and char rather than burn to ashes.

To turn the ore into iron, huge blast furnaces were constructed from native sandstone and lined with clay bricks. Chunks of raw iron ore, charcoal, and limestone were dropped into the open tops of the furnaces from

You won't see many other mountain bikers at Pine Creek.

wooden buildings surrounding them. When the charcoal was ignited, air was forced through the sides of the furnace, blasting the charcoal with oxygen to feed the fire. As the mixture of ore and limestone melted, the pure iron flowed from the furnace and was molded into blocks. This "pig iron" was then loaded onto railcars destined for foundries in Cincinnati, Cleveland, the East Coast, and even Europe.

MilesDirections

0.0 START at the trailhead about a quarter of a mile off OH 93 on Telegraph Hill Road.

0.3 Turn left at the three-way intersection. The trail to the right dead-ends.

1.3 Continue straight on the main trail following the trail markers.

2.1 Turn left on the little spur trail.

2.2 Arrive at the main trail again and turn left.

2.8 Continue straight. There is an overlook off to the right.

3.0 The downhill goes through a stand of pine trees.

3.3 Cross the gravel road and the wooden bridge.

3.5 Continue straight following the trail markers.

3.7 Go right when the trail forks.

5.1 The trail turns left (follow the trail markers).

5.9 Cross a wooden bridge after a big downhill.

6.1 Turn around at the gravel road and retrace your tracks.

12.2 End the ride at the parking lot.

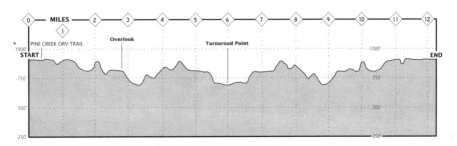

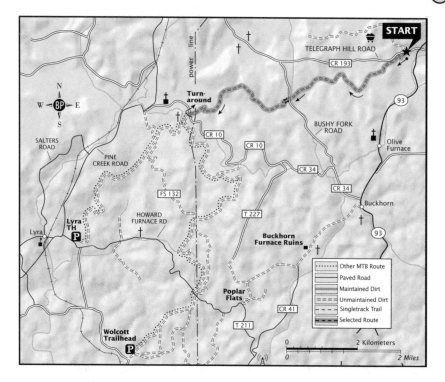

89

Ride Information

Trail Contact:
Wayne National Forest
Ironton Ranger District
Pedro, OH
(614) 532-3223

Schedule:
April 15 to November 15

Cost:
The Wayne National Forest is a fee area. Trail passes can be purchased for $5 at Forest Service headquarters in Pedro.

Local Information:
Portsmouth Convention and Visitors Bureau
Portsmouth, OH
(740) 353-1116

Accommodations:
Wayne National Forest
(primitive camping)
Vesuvius Recreation Area
Pedro, OH
(614) 532-3223

Maps:
USGS maps: Pedro, OH; South Greer, OH

Hanging Rock iron, as it was called, earned a reputation around the world for its strength and resistance to rust and corrosion. By 1850, 22 furnaces in the area produced 56,000 tons of iron annually ranking Ohio second in the nation in iron production. The region's iron helped create the nation's railroad industry and by 1860 Ohio had more railroad track than any other state in the Union. When the Civil War broke out, the industry changed focus and contributed tons of iron to make cannons for the Union army.

But the prosperity of the Ohio iron industry would not last. By the late 1870s the forests used to make charcoal were all but gone. Competition from Lake Superior ore and efficient coal-fired furnaces in Cleveland and Youngstown put many local operations out of business. By 1878 only half of the state's furnaces remained. Today, outdoor enthusiasts are in luck: There are only a few crumbling furnaces left in the state and the forest has been replanted.

The trains that carried the iron probably traveled through these hills much faster than mountain bikes do today, but that fact doesn't mean the trails at Pine Creek are slow. The trail detailed below begins on top of a ridge and travels gradually downhill from there. The first descent can be very fast. The second downhill is steeper with tighter turns, so it's a good idea to slow down. The return trip, obviously, is not as fast as the way out. Nor is it painstakingly slow as the trail climbs gradually and lacks any real technical challenges. This helps the trail speed along and seem almost fast. The only obstacles mountain bikers must deal with are motorized dirt bikes and the deep ruts they leave on the trail.

The Pine Creek trail system is arranged like three fingers branching off from each other at a central point. This means that loop rides are next to impossible without a lengthy ride along the road to link each trail. The length of the trails also makes riding from one trailhead to another prohibitive. Those with time should consider shuttling a car to another trailhead for a nice long ride. Otherwise, ride out one way, then turn around when you tire and head back for home.

ORV (Off-Road Vehicle) Trails

Undeniably, the Wayne National Forest is one of the best places in the state (and probably the whole Midwest) to ride off-road. Mountain bikers know this, but so do thousands of motocrossers and four wheelers. Every weekend, and especially during holidays, they flock to the Wayne as the trails become an off-road highway.

But just because machines weighing ten times more than yours are being propelled through the woods at high speed doesn't mean you have to avoid these trails. If you can get over the occasional noxious fumes put off by these machines, you can enjoy riding here any time. There are just a few things you need to know to make the experience safer and more enjoyable.

- Because you are sharing these trails with motorized vehicles, you should act as if you are using any other street, road, or alley where you would encounter vehicles. It may sound simple enough, but make sure to always pass oncoming traffic on the right.

- Listen up. ORV's make a considerable amount of noise and you will have plenty of warning when they are coming up on you. Leave the headphones at home.

- When you do meet an ORV or a group of them, pull off to the side of the trail and wait for them to pass. They are much bigger than you, both in weight and width. The inconvenience of stopping is only slight, as such encounters only last a couple of seconds.

- Use hand signals. You will immediately notice that ORV riders hold up their hands signaling how many are following in their group. You should do the same to protect everyone involved.

- Obey all traffic laws. Some of the trails use gravel roads to connect and have posted speed limits. Many trails are marked as closed and some of the roads are closed to all traffic other than cars and trucks. The rangers are very particular about riding on the roads and will issue tickets.

With these tips and a little common sense, you should have no problems when riding ORV trails. Most users of these trails are very courteous and slow down when approaching oncoming traffic. The trails are very wide and facilitate easy passing. In many cases they are amazed that a person on a bike can climb the huge hills and descend faster than the cumbersome four-wheelers. Conflicts rarely arise, and the tips included here are merely cautionary.

10 Bob Evans Farm

Ride Summary

Though the ride listed here is only three miles long, there are about 15 miles of trails at Bob Evans Farm, and all are open to mountain biking. The climbs are often steep, but the descents and fast ridgeline trails make the effort well worth it. The main trails are marked—Gatewood is orange, Adamsville is yellow, Wood is blue. These trails also intersect several horse trails that are not color coded, but which are very fun to ride. To extend the rides you must pass through gates to reach trails on the other side of the pastures. Make sure you close the gates behind you so the cattle don't escape.

Ride Specs

County: Galia County
Start: The log-cabin village of Adamsville, east of the gift shop
Length: 3 miles; 15 miles total
Approximate Riding Time: 45 minutes
Difficulty Rating: Moderate to difficult due to steep climbs and loose, rocky descents
Trail Types: Singletrack and horse trails
Lay of the Land: Steep and rocky bridle and hiking trails with some open fields
Elevation Gain: 374 feet
Land Status: Private
Nearest Town: Rio Grande
Other Trail Users: Hikers and equestrians

Getting There

From Rio Grande: Drive east on OH 588 for about one mile. Bob Evans Farm is on the left side of the road and is marked by large signs. You can't miss it. Park at the log-cabin village of Adamsville before the river. *DeLorme: Ohio Atlas & Gazetteer.* Page 86, B-3

There are about 15 miles of trails on Bob Evans' 1,100-acre farm in tiny Rio Grande, Ohio, but they can never match the miles and miles of sausage that the humble farmer produces every year. While Evans owns more than 400 restaurants today, he has never forgotten his roots and has opened his farm for everyone to use. Today, in addition to mountain biking, he offers hourly horseback riding, canoeing, evening hayrides, overnight canoe excursions, and combined canoe and horseback camping.

Evans' first restaurant, which he opened in 1946, was a 12-stool diner open 24 hours a day along Ohio Route 7 in Gallipolis. Eggs and toast were

the diner's specialty because most of the truckers who frequented it wanted breakfast. When it was cold enough for meat not to spoil, Evans served fresh sausage sandwiches.

After Evans picked up a secondhand refrigerator in 1948 he was able to serve sausage year-round. Soon he was selling sausage all over the state. In 1968 the first restaurant in the Bob Evans chain opened in Chillicothe. Today, the $800 million company is publicity traded on NASDAQ with more than 400 Bob Evans restaurants across the nation.

Evans' generous sense of community means some great riding for off-road cyclists. The trails are deep in the hills of southeast Ohio, so lung-busting climbs are the norm. The trails here climb immediately from the trailhead on Cora Road. Warming up is not really an option. But the extensive views of Rio Grande and the surrounding valleys from the top of the hill are reason enough to stop and rest. These views are thought to be the first Daniel Boone had during his westward quest in the 1700s. Boone spent two winters in a cave along Raccoon Creek, which runs through Bob Evans Farm not far from where the ride begins.

MilesDirections

0.0 START from the pioneer cabins past the main farm buildings.

0.3 The trailhead turns right from the gravel road. Follow the Gatewood Trail to the right.

0.6 At the top of the hill the trail goes across a field to the woods. The trail intersection is behind the fallen tree. Go right.

0.7 Go right again at the intersection and descend a loose, rocky trail.

0.9 Turn left at the pasture fence.

1.1 After a small ravine go right on the horse trail.

1.3 Turn left and begin to climb.

1.4 At the top of the hill turn right.

1.8 Turn left after the Gatewood signs.

1.9 Turn left and climb.

2.1 Turn left onto the horse trail.

2.2 Turn left again then take an immediately right onto the Gatewood Trail.

2.4 Turn right through the field and head back down toward the trailhead.

2.7 At the road turn left for the short ride back to the start.

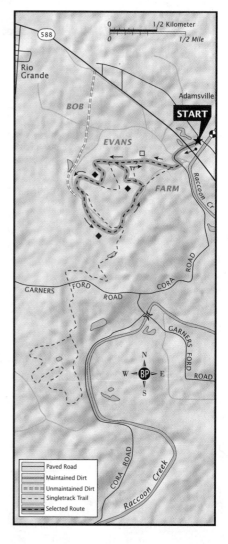

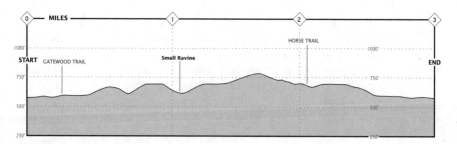

Ride Information

📞 Trail Contact:
Bob Evans Farm
Rio Grande, OH
1-800-994-FARM

🕐 Schedule:
Call ahead to ensure there is no conflicting events.

💡 Local Events/Attractions:
Bob Evans Farm Festival
Rio Grande, OH
1-800-994-FARM

🛏 Accommodations:
Bob Evans Farm
Rio Grande, OH
1-800-994-FARM

🗺 Maps:
USGS maps: Patriot, OH; Rodney, OH

When a River is still a Creek

Raccoon Creek is the longest creek in the world. A creek is defined as any channel of water being less then one hundred miles long. At the time it was measured, Raccoon Creek was determined to be 99 miles long. Later it was discovered to be longer, but it is still defined as a creek.

Like the climbs, the descents at Bob Evans Farm are steep. Some sections are loose and rocky, while others provide little stopping room before the creeks at the bottom. The best sections, however, are the ridge tops. These trails are fast, gently twisting, and a blast to ride.

The clay soil on the farm can be treacherous after a heavy rain, so it's best to avoid riding here in the early spring. Most of the trails are multiple-use and get quite a bit of horse traffic. Unlike some bridle trails, however, they are well maintained and free of hoof craters. Just watch for manure. Trail markings are not that great in some places, but getting lost isn't too much of a problem as all of the trails run north-south. Some of the trails pass through fenced-in pastures and hay fields. Go ahead and pass through the gates, but mind your manners and make sure you close the gates behind you. If the hay is being cut, just stay in the woods. The friendly people at the visitor's station will enlighten you with the trail conditions and can give you a map.

The ride begins at the historic log-cabin village of Adamsville, the area's original settlement. Welsh settlers came to the area in 1818 after their boat washed away in a storm along the Ohio River. Legend holds that, during the storm, the women in the group, refusing to travel the remaining 175 miles west after an extremely arduous transatlantic journey, cut the ropes mooring the boat. The Welsh travelers were stuck without a boat, so the men quickly found jobs constructing a new highway from Centerville to Jackson.

While working, the landscape reminded them so much of their native Wales that they decided to stay for good.

By 1836 fellow Welshmen began populating the region in significant numbers. Ten years later there were enough people in the area to require a post office. Up to this point the growing little settlement was known as Adamsville, so-named after its founder, Adam Rickabaugh. But when they registered the name with the post office, they discovered that another Ohio town had already claimed the name. A new name would have to be found. One of the townspeople, reading about the fighting along the Rio Grande in Texas, came up with an idea, and all the townspeople agreed that Rio Grande would be a fine name. Unfortunately, no one here had ever heard Spanish spoken before, and pronounced their new name "Rye-O-Grand." The pronunciation stands to this day.

Daniel Boone lived nearby here.

Survey Marker Trail

Ride Summary

The Survey Marker ride starts where almost every ride in Athens begins-the Monument, a stone spire on the college green surrounded by statues of Civil War soldiers. After winding through town, riders follow the Hocking River Rail Trail through some of the most scenic valley terrain in southeast Ohio. After a nice warm-up on the paved trail, things get steep very quickly. The climb is demanding, but mellows out at the top of the ridge. All that climbing is worth it, though, as the return descent is a blast. On the way back to Athens stop in at Miller's Chicken for the best fried chicken in town.

Ride Specs

Start: Monument on the Ohio University green
Length: 15.4 miles
Approximate Riding Time: 2 hours
Difficulty Rating: Moderate to difficult due to steep and rocky climbs
Trail Surface: Paved bike path, double-track, and singletrack
Lay of the Land: Flat bike path and a doubletrack climb
Elevation Gain: 757 feet
Land Status: Public and power company right-of-ways
Nearest City: Athens
Other Trail Users: Hunters and off-road vehicles

Getting There

From Athens: Head north and up the hill on Richland Avenue from the football stadium (just off the Richland Avenue exit on OH 33). Turn left at the light onto Court Street. At the next light, on the right, is the Monument-the starting point of the ride. It's nearly impossible to find a parking space in Athens, and traffic cops are everywhere, so look for a spot away from uptown and pedal your way back the start. *DeLorme: Ohio Atlas & Gazetteer.* Page 80, B-1

The city of Athens and the surrounding area have been somewhat of a cycling Mecca in the state of Ohio for years. The city first secured this status with the rise in popularity of road cycling in the early 1980s. Athens was a stop along the grueling Race Across America (RAAM) during the event's early years. The Brick Criterium, famous for its cobblestones, climbs, and treacherous corners, has attracted names like pro cycling legend Greg LeMond, pro road teams 7-Eleven and Coors Light, and other national-caliber competitors. But only in the past few years has Athens put itself on the off-road bicycling map. Races like the

The scenery alone makes this ride worthwhile.

Di Di Mau in Nelsonville, 15 minutes to the north, have helped make this area a new off-road destination. Despite these high-profile competitions, however, most would argue that it's the beautifully hilly terrain that really draws the riders.

While much of Ohio is typical Midwestern flatland, the southeast portion of the state and especially the Athens area are almost like different worlds. About 350 million years ago the region was part of a vast sea. Beneath this sea sand was cementing itself into the sandstone that now forms most of the region's bedrock and cliffs. At the same time, volcanic forces to the east were forming the Appalachian Mountains and, subsequently, the hills surrounding Athens. Today these hills are full of lush vegetation, wildlife, and excellent riding terrain.

There are probably hundreds of miles of trails in the hills surrounding Athens, and most of them see very little traffic. Most cyclists in Athens are Ohio University students transplanted from other parts of the state to go school for few years. Consequently, they often know very little about what the area has to offer and don't venture very far from home base.

MilesDirections

0.0 START from the Monument on the college green. Turn right on Court Street, ride two blocks, then turn left on West State. At the bottom of the hill take a pass through the light then turn right on Central. Follow Central until it dead-ends at Frank's Bait Shop. (This is your last chance to pick up any food or beverage items you may want before you continue to the middle of nowhere.) Take a left. Immediately on your right is Currier. Go down the hill and turn right on the bike path. Take the bike path for several miles.

5.5 Cross Route 682 then continue on Hamlee Road. This gravel road follows the Hocking River.

6.5 Pass a log cabin on the left. At this point the road ends and the trail begins.

6.9 The trail turns to the left and prepares for its long ascent. Watch out for the deep mud holes at the bottom of the hill. It's best to get off and walk.

7.0 Shift down and settle in for the long climb.

7.2 Stage two of the climb. This one is a little steeper, a little more technical. Be prepared for ruts, roots, and loose rocks.

7.3 The trail levels out a bit here. Soon, however, it twists right then left into another steep and even more difficult climb. There is a big rut in the middle of the trail and there are lots of loose rocks.

7.3 You have reached the top of the ridge when you see three pink ribbons around a tree. Twist left around this tree and you'll be rewarded with a gentle, twisting downhill through the foliage. You are still on top of the ridge.

7.5 Use your momentum to get you going up this short climb that takes you to the right of the ridge top.

7.7 The trail bends left then cuts to the right up the final climb of the ride. There are roots on the trail and the sandstone is loose, but there's no need to be picky about lines. At the top you will see a survey marker. You can continue past this point for about another mile before running into Poston Road near the Plains, but it is recommended that you turn around and enjoy the fruits of your labor. Just catch your breath, chant the words "gravity is my friend" over and over, then bomb down the hill with a huge grin on your face.

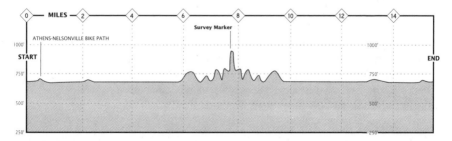

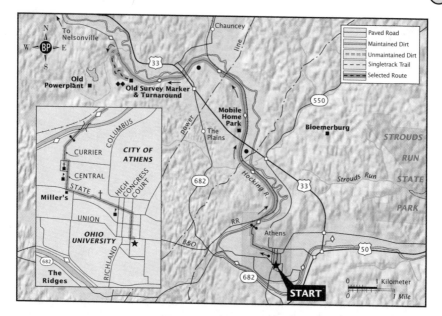

Ride Information

Trail Contact:
Ohio University Mountain Bike Club
Athens, OH
biking@oak.cats.ohiou.edu
www.oak.cats.ohiou.edu/~biking/

Schedule:
Open year-round

Local Information:
**Athens County Convention
and Visitor's Bureau**
Athens, OH
1-800-878-9767

Local Events/Attractions:
Di Di Mau Mountain Bike Race
Athens County Convention
and Visitor's Bureau
Athens, OH
1-800-878-9767

Restaurant:
Miller's Chicken
Athens, OH
(740) 593-6544

Local Bike Shops:
Athens Bicycle
Athens, OH
(740) 594-9944

Cycle Path
Athens, OH
(740) 593-8482

Pedaler & the Packer
Athens, OH
1-888-946-3483
(740) 592-4630

Maps:
USGS maps: Athens, OH; Jacksonville, OH; Nelsonville, OH; The Plains, OH

Not so with the Survey Marker Trail-at least not if you're a member of the Ohio University Mountain Bike Club. The Survey Marker Trail was cut years ago as an ORV path. It gets its name from the old survey marker that greets riders at the top of the climb. To this day it remains one of those local treasures among the Athens off-road scene.

In keeping with the tradition of the Ohio University Mountain Bike Club this ride begins at the monument on the college green. The club is *the* scene for cyclists in Athens, meeting every day for a ride. All levels of cyclists show up, from state champions to mere beginners, and nobody ever feels left out. While novices may not be able to hang with the local experts, the general companionship allows knowledge of the local trails to be passed along for future generations of riders looking for a good place to ride.

If you ride with the club you will wind through town and then jump on the Athens-Nelsonville Bike Path for approximately six miles. Don't worry, though-the path is flat and the scenery along the Hocking River is wonderful. Besides, the approach is a great warm-up for the grueling climb ahead. And then the fun will begin.

Snake Hollow ORV Trail

Ride Summary

Of the 65 miles of trails in the Monday Creek ORV Area, the Snake Hollow Loop is probably the easiest to navigate. While the Dorr Run Loop is the area's most popular trail, Snake Hollow sees less traffic and has fewer climbs. The six-mile loop climbs quite a bit, but every long ascent is rewarded with a blisteringly fast downhill. In fact, Snake Hollow has what may be the best downhill in the Monday Creek trail system. Much of the trail traverses a ridge, so speeds are constant and the jumps are less intimidating than those in other sections of the Wayne National Forest. Beware of water bars, however. They can ruin an inattentive cyclist's day. Adventurous (and fit) riders can pedal from Snake Hollow to Dorr Run for a ride of nearly 30 miles.

Ride Specs

Start: From the parking lot on Buchtel Road
Length: 6.1 miles; 65 miles of trails total
Approximate Riding Time: 1 hour
Difficulty: Moderate to difficult due to two steep, long climbs and many jumps
Trail Surface: ORV doubletrack
Lay of the Land: Rocky and hilly
Elevation Gain: 679 feet
Land Status: National forest
Nearest Town: Nelsonville
Other Trail Users: Hunters and off-road vehicles

Getting There

From Columbus: Head south on U.S. 33. Turn left on OH 78 in Nelsonville. Drive approximately two miles then turn left again at Carbon Hill-Buchtel Road. After about a quarter of a mile the road veers left at a four-way stop and becomes Buchtel Road. Do not make a sharp left or you will end up back in Nelsonville. The parking lot for the Main Corridor/Snake Hollow Trails is on the right. The Snake Hollow Trail is on the left (west) side of the road. *DeLorme: Ohio Atlas & Gazetteer.* Page 80, A-1

From Athens: Head north on U.S. 33 toward Nelsonville for approximately 10 miles. Turn right on OH 78 in Nelsonville. Follow the directions above.

The crash of the New York Stock Exchange in 1929 launched a worldwide economic depression that spelled disaster for southeast Ohio. The region's farmers were most affected. Years of neglect left their land eroded and infertile, and market conditions would not support the few products that they had to offer. Destitute, unemployed, and unable to pay their taxes, these farmers left to work in factories in nearby cities or joined mining and lumber crews to make what little money they could.

Bricks are very slippery when wet.

This mass migration left millions of acres of tax-delinquent land and a state government that was in need of revenue. As a result, the federal government purchased the lands and declared them a national forest. Today this land constitutes more than 210,000 acres in the rugged hills of the Appalachian foothills.

The Wayne National Forest has a wealth of history, most of which is associated with its abundance of resources. At the turn of the century much of the local economy revolved around the vast clay deposits found in the surrounding hills. Communities in southeast Ohio were famous for the bricks made from this clay. They produced the finest bricks in the world, and many can still be found in the streets and sidewalks inscribed with the names of the southeastern Ohio foundries from which they came. But this industry would also fade, leaving the economy to once again suffer.

More recently, coal mining has left its mark on the region. Before the implementation of the Clean Air Act, southeast Ohio communities exported their high-sulfur coal. Mining companies were free to strip huge tracts of land to reach the valuable coal deposits. Evidence of this strip mining still exists and is visible in many spots along the trails of the

MilesDirections

0.0 START at the trailhead on Buchtel Road. The Snake Hollow Trail heads west from the parking lot.

0.4 Turn left at the fork and follow the Main Corridor Trail up the hill. Do not follow the Creek Trail to the right.

0.6 Continue straight up the hill following the Main Corridor Trail. Again, do not take the right fork.

0.7 Turn right, following the trail marker (orange triangle with a dot in the middle).

0.9 At the top of the hill go right, following the Snake Hollow Trail.

2.5 Pass a gas well.

2.8 Turn left after a short and rocky climb.

3.0 Follow the Snake Hollow Trail to the left (the trail to the right goes to Dorr Run).

4.3 At the bottom of the hill go left.

4.8 Begin a long climb to the left. This is the last climb of the Snake Hollow Loop.

5.1 At the top of the hill go straight, following signs for the Main Corridor. You are now doubling back.

5.4 Turn left and continue to follow the Main Corridor Trail.

5.5 Turn right, following the Main Corridor Trail.

6.1 Finish back at the parking lot.

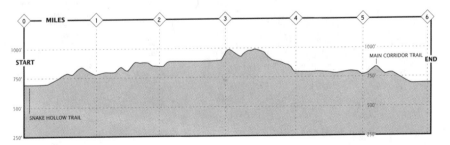

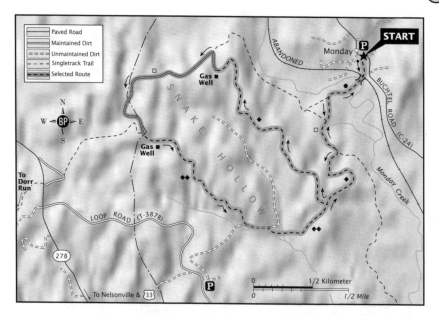

Paved Road
Maintained Dirt
Unmaintained Dirt
Singletrack Trail
Selected Route

Gas Well

SNAKE HOLLOW

Gas Well

To Dorr Run

LOOP ROAD (T-387B)

278

To Nelsonville & 33

ABANDONED

Monday

START

P

BUCHTEL ROAD (C-24)

Monday Creek

P

0   1/2 Kilometer
0   1/2 Mile

Extreme riding, Ohio style.

Ride Information

Trail Contacts:
Wayne National Forest
Athens Ranger District
Athens, OH
(614) 592-6644

Schedule:
April 15 to November 15

Fees/Permits:
The Wayne National Forest is a fee area. Trail passes can be purchased for $5 at forest headquarters in Athens or at any bike shop in Athens.

Local Information:
Athens County Convention and Visitors Bureau
Athens, OH
1-800-878-9767

Local Attractions:
Hocking Hills State Park
Logan, OH
(740) 385-6841
Offers incredible hiking and rock climbing

Accommodations:
Strouds Run State Park (camping)
Athens, OH
(740) 592-2302

Wayne National Forest (camping)
Athens, OH
(614) 592-6644

Local Bike Shops:
Athens Bicycle
Athens, OH
(740) 592-9944

Cycle Path
Athens, OH
(740) 593-8482

Pedaler & the Packer
Athens, OH
1-888-9-GO-DIVE
pedaler@frognet.net

Maps:
USGS map: Nelsonville, OH

FYI...

In 1884 the New Straightsville Mines were set on fire by angry miners. It could burn for centuries.

Wayne. On Dorr Run an old mining road paved with century-old bricks still remains. On Snake Hollow there is a huge clearing where the soil is still black from an old slag heap. Some of the streams and swamps still run orange from acidic runoff. The water is definitely not safe for drinking, and is probably not great for cleaning bike frames either.

Today the Wayne National Forest continues to provide many resources for public consumption. Mining still exists, but environmental standards ensure that the land is returned to its original condition. Gas and oil wells dot the landscape, and logging is a big business.

If it were up to environmentalists, however, none of this would go on in the Wayne. In recent years they have been outraged by the policies of the National Forest Service and have attended congressional hearings, held town meetings, and picketed Forest Service offices. They feel like they have no say in Forest Service policies that control such activities as mining and logging. Some environmentalists have even suggested that the land be completely shut off to all human activity, including hiking, hunting, off-road driving, and mountain biking.

Meanwhile, Congress and the Forest Service have stuck to their policy of designating these lands for use by the public, including the timber and mining interests. As a result, hundreds of thousands of people continue to visit the Wayne every year.

Bermed turns make this downhill very fast.

Long Ridge

Ride Summary

With its fast and scary descents and steep, hallucination-inducing climbs, the Long Ridge Trail leaves many riders with their heads spinning. The trail never looks the same and is one of the most difficult in the state to navigate. A compass and a topographic map are absolutely necessary for newcomers. Still, the trails are a blast to ride and are much less crowded than the neighboring Dorr Run and Main Corridor Trails.

Ride Specs

Start: From the sign for the Long Ridge Trail on OH 78
Length: 9.1-mile loop of 65 miles total
Approximate Riding Time: 2 hours
Difficulty Rating: Difficult due to steep climbs and descents
Trail Surface: ORV doubletrack and gravel roads
Lay of the Land: Rocky and hilly
Elevation Gain: 1,057 feet
Land Status: National forest
Nearest Town: Nelsonville
Other Trail Users: ORVs and hunters

Getting There

From Nelsonville: Follow OH 78 east toward Murray City. The gravel road to the Long Ridge Trail is on the left side of OH 78, about three miles past Buchtel. The road can be difficult to navigate in a car, so this ride starts at the bottom of the obvious hill. If you have a four-wheel drive vehicle you can start at the parking area (mile 2.1) and skip the mile-long climb to the trail. *DeLorme: Ohio Atlas & Gazetteer.* Page 80, A-1

I t's easy to get lost in the Wayne National Forest, especially when riding the Long Ridge Trail. The multiple twists, turns, ups, and downs are very disorienting. In fact, it's common to ride in circles without realizing it, primarily because the trail is so fast that it's difficult to pay attention to landmarks.

One landmark that is hard to miss, however, is Mount Nebo, which lies to the south and is one of the highest peaks in Athens County. The mountain (really a hill, but large when compared to those in other parts of the state) has been considered haunted since the late 1840s when a group known as the Spiritualists settled around it, believing it to be a source of psychic energy and an ideal place to communicate with the dead.

The area includes other spiritual stomping grounds as well. Not far from Long Ridge lies the Hanning Cemetery, one of five cemeteries that surround the city of Athens. When connected, the cemeteries form a pentagram. According to pagan tradition, a pentagram is a protective force and

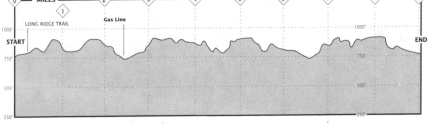

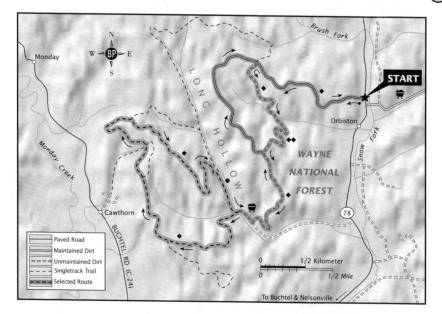

MilesDirections

0.0 START at the bottom of the hill across from the gravel road to the Long Ridge Trail.

1.0 Go left at the trail marked with an orange diamond and white circle.

1.3 Stay left along the bottom of a gully.

1.7 Switchback down to the clearing.

1.8 Go left up the hill.

1.9 Turn left at the top of the hill.

2.0 Go straight (following the trail markers).

2.1 The trail hits the gravel road and turns left after the campsite (following the orange diamond/white circle markers).

2.5 Follow the gas line straight.

3.0 At the bottom of the hill go right, then go left where the trail splits.

3.4 Go left at the top of the hill (following the orange diamond).

3.6 Turn right at the three-way intersection.

3.9 Turn right (following the orange diamond/white circle markers).

4.1 Take the downhill to the left.

4.3 At the four-way intersection go straight.

4.8 Go right (following trail markers).

5.7 Turn left along the top of the ridge.

5.9 Go right (following trail markers), then go right again at the bottom of the hill.

6.0 Go straight.

6.9 Turn left at the gravel road.

7.0 At the parking lot take a right onto the gravel road.

9.1 End of the ride.

Ride Information

Trail Contact:
Wayne National Forest
Athens Ranger District
Athens, OH
(614) 592-6644

☉ Schedule:
April 15 to November 15

⑤ Fees/Permits:
The Wayne National Forest is a fee area. Trail passes can be purchased for $5 at Forest Service headquarters or at any bike shop in Athens.

❷ Local Information:
Athens County Convention and Visitors Bureau
Athens, OH
1-800-878-9767

⊜ Accommodations:
Strouds Run State Park
(primitive camping)
Wayne National Forest
Athens, OH
(740) 592-2302

⊕ Local Bike Shops:
Athens Bicycle
Athens, OH
(740) 594-9944
athensbicycle@eurekanet.net

Cycle Path
Athens, OH
(740) 593-8482

Pedaler & the Packer
Athens, OH
1-888-9-GO-DIVE
pedaler@frognet.net

❶ Maps:
USGS map: Nelsonville, OH

its center a safe zone for paranormal activity. As luck would have it, the center of this particular pentagram happens to be Ohio University. As you might imagine, numerous tales of strange encounters have come from buildings and dormitories across the school's campus.

Another prominent haunting tale surrounds the nearby Moonville train tunnel. Locals and visitors alike have seen a number of ghosts in the tunnel, said to be the spirits of several people hit by trains. Train conductors, too, claim to have seen a figure swinging a lantern back and forth in an apparent effort to get them to stop.

If all the spirits in the area don't cause you to lose your mind as you ride the Long Ridge Trail, then perhaps one of the very long and steep climbs or the many roots, ruts, and rocks will. In any event, expect to finish this ride in an exceptionally ragged state—both physically and mentally.

Sausage and Roasted Pepper Penne

6 red peppers, quartered
6 tablespoons olive oil
Salt, pepper
Sprinkle oregano and thyme
1 large package of mushrooms
1 cup fresh parsley
2 cloves garlic
1 lb. Bob Evans Italian Sausage (see chapter 10)
1 cup reserved cooking liquid

Heat oven to 450°.
Roast peppers with 3 tablespoons oil and salt and pepper. Bake until edges are dark.
Mix oregano, parsley, thyme and garlic together and set aside.
Add 3 tablespoons oil to the skillet and cook mushrooms until tender.
Add herb/garlic mixture and salt and pepper to mushrooms and set aside.
Cook sausage over medium heat until brown. Drain.
Combine sausage, mushrooms and peppers in a baking dish and cover with foil.
Warm in oven on lowest temperature.
Cook penne and keep 1 cup of the liquid.
Combine ingredients in a large bowl and stir. Add cheese.

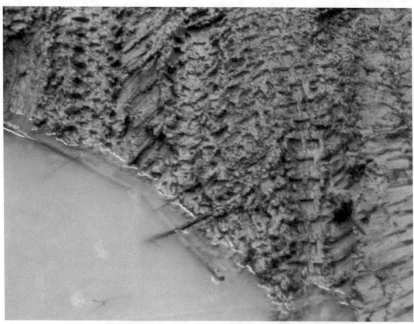

Hocking clay sticks like glue.

14   Perry State Forest

Ride Summary

Perry State Forest, with its precipitous drops and big jumps, can be a roller-coaster playground for mountain bikers. All of the trails are technically and physically challenging, but some flatter and faster trails even things out. The mud here can be very bad, so stay away when it rains.

Ride Specs

Start: Perry State Forest trailhead parking lot on FS 154

Length: Approximately 13 miles of interconnecting loops

Approximate Riding Time: 2 hours

Difficulty Rating: Difficult due to steep climbs and loose, rocky descents, and big drop-offs

Trail Surface: Doubletrack

Lay of the Land: Old mining sites and forest

Land Status: State forest

Nearest Town: New Lexington

Other Trail Users: ORVs and hunters

Getting There

From Columbus: Take I-70 west for about 30 miles to OH 13. Drive south on OH 13 to the town of New Lexington, then take OH 345 north for about six miles. The trailhead is on FS 154, just past the Forest Service headquarters. *DeLorme: Ohio Atlas & Gazetteer.* Page 70, B-1

I n some places the wide doubletrack paths of Perry State Forest are more like roads than trails. You can thank motorized traffic, in the form of dirt bikes and four-wheelers, for that. You can also thank our high-horsepower friends for the deep ruts that fill with rainwater to form tire-sucking mud holes. The mud here is horrific—the clay clogs up everything and can make spinning your wheels next to impossible.

Despite the mud and the ruts, however, Perry's trails can be a blast to ride. For one, motorcyclists like to make trails that go straight up and down. While such drop-ins may be intimidating, you'll never forget how it feels to fly down their precipitous walls.

To the east of the parking area is a large open space with lots of jumps and half-pipe-type riding. Riders could easily spend an hour here just playing around. Rushing down a steep hill and then launching up another creates a sensation like that of riding a roller coaster. There isn't much vegetation here; in fact, the landscape is often described as "lunar."

The land is scarred, but fun to play on.

Other areas further away from the beginning of the trail system are more like singletrack than roads. Highly recommended is the six-mile Red Loop, on the northwest side of the forest. The terrain here includes abundant jumps, rocks, berms, and tree roots. The riding is fast in places, but there are a number of hills that may require you to walk or carry your bike.

Just a few miles north of Perry State Forest is the historic National Road, which, when it was first built almost 200 years ago as a link to the Western

Ride Information

 Trail Contact:
Perry State Forest
New Lexington, OH
(740) 674-4035

Schedule:
Closed December 1 to March 31

Local Information:
Perry County Development/
Tourism Center
Zanesville, OH
1-800-343-7379

Local Events:
Velo-Z mountain bike races
Loudonville, OH
(740) 674-4297

Accommodations:
Perry County Development/
Tourism Center
Zanesville, OH
1-800-343-7379

Local Bike Shop:
Wheel & Spoke Bike Shop
Zanesville, OH
(740) 453-3438

Maps:
USGS map: Fultonham, OH

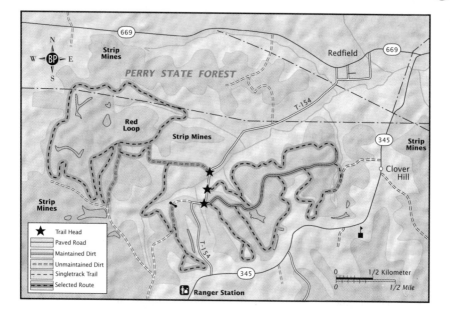

MilesDirections

While the trails are marked in places, there certainly could be better signs. Trails branch off everywhere, so a specific route cannot be recommended. Just go and have fun and spend as much time as you can exploring this trail system.

frontier, would have been fantastic for mountain biking. The National Road was an engineering marvel. It had a slope no steeper than 5 percent, a 66-foot right-of-way, and was 20 feet wide and covered with stone and earth. The road's 12-inch stone foundation eliminated the deep, muddy ruts that made other roads impassible in the spring.

The road was originally designed to extend to the Mississippi River, but a quarrel between Illinois and Missouri and a shortage of funding put an end to it. Those in Missouri wanted the crossing at St. Louis, while the people in Illinois wanted the crossing further to the south. The road, which today is known as U.S. Route 40, only made it as far as Vandalia, then the capital of Illinois.

15

River View Trail

Ride Summary

The River View Trail is one of the few singletrack trails in Ohio that is on national forest land but open to mountain bikes. The ride starts out with a long and steep climb but then settles down on rolling singletrack, doubletrack, and dirt roads. A technical descent marks the ride's end.

Ride Specs

Start: Leith Run Campground
Length: 11.2-mile out-and-back
Approximate Riding Time: 2 hours
Difficulty Rating: Difficult due to steep climbs and rocky descents
Trail Surface: Singletrack, doubletrack, and dirt roads
Lay of the Land: Hilly and wooded
Elevation Gain: 634 feet
Land Status: National forest
Nearest Town: Marietta, OH
Other Trail Users: Hikers and hunters

Getting There

From Marietta: Head northeast on OH 7. The Leith Run Campground and Picnic Area is about six miles past the village of Newport on the right side of the road. *DeLorme: Ohio Atlas & Gazetteer.* Page 73, D-7

lthough Marietta was one of the first settlements in Ohio, it was one of the last places in the state to be discovered by mountain bikers. Unlike other areas of the state, though, that have taken an anti-bike stance, the Marietta District of the Wayne National Forest has opened all of its trails to bikes. And unlike other national forest lands in Ohio, the trails in the Marietta District are almost all singletrack.

Miles and miles of well-mapped singletrack snake through the hills of the Marietta District. This is probably the only trail system in the state that has been mapped so extensively. But just because the trails are well mapped doesn't mean they are easy to get to.

Of all the trails in the Marietta District of the Wayne National Forest, the River View Trail is the easiest to access (via Ohio Route 7, which parallels the Ohio River). This is an important thing, because the trails further north can be hard to find, thanks to poorly marked and steep and muddy dirt roads. There are good facilities at the start of the trail at the Leith Run picnic/boat launch area. The campground is fairly modern with running

water and bathroom facilities, and is a good place to launch a weekend of riding in the Wayne National Forest.

After a short jaunt along the river, the trail crosses Ohio Route 7 and immediately begins climbing. This climb is not for the timid at heart. There are approximately 15 switchbacks ascending the hill as it climbs steeply from the river valley. Much of it must be walked. But don't worry—the trails on the ridge are worth the suffering.

The trail at the top of the climb is a welcome relief. It rolls along the ridge with a couple of short climbs and gradual descents. The ridge-top trail begins as singletrack, then turns to doubletrack and finally to a gated dirt road. The area's trails drain pretty well by Ohio standards (there is no thick clay), but this road is a different story. There is very little rock here to keep

Ride Information

Trail Contact:
Wayne National Forest
Athens, OH
(740) 592-6644

Schedule:
Closed December 15 to April 15

Local Information:
Marietta/Washington County
Convention & Visitors Bureau
Marietta, OH
1-888-659-7968

Local Attraction:
Campus Martius Museum
Marietta, OH
(614) 373-3750

Accommodations:
Marietta/Washington County
Convention and Visitors Bureau
Marietta, OH
1-888-659-7968

Maps:
USGS map: Raven Rock, OH

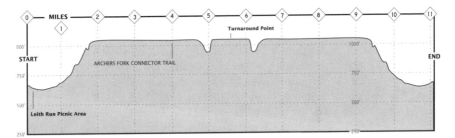

MilesDirections

0.0 START at the Leith Run Campground.

0.1 Turn right onto the singletrack where the paved trail splits.

0.5 Cross OH 7.

0.6 Go right up the hill.

1.2 The trail splits at the top of a ridge after many switchbacks. Go right.

1.5 Go straight along the ridge then veer left and uphill.

2.4 Go right (following trail markers), continuing along the ridge.

2.7 The singletrack turns into a dirt road. Continue straight.

3.1 Continue straight at the fork.

3.9 Continue straight along the gravel road when you get to the gate.

4.0 Cross a paved road and join the singletrack trail called Archer's Fork Connector.

4.6 Descend an excellent downhill to a creek, then cross the creek.

4.8 Follow the switchbacks up the hill.

5.6 Turn around and retrace the route back to the start.

11.2 Arrive at Leith Run Campground and the end of the ride.

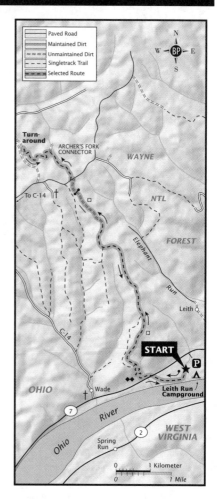

things firm and the mud can be thick when it rains. When it's dry, the road is probably the fastest section of this ride.

After crossing a paved road, the trail turns back to singletrack and a long, technical descent dips in and out of a creek bed. The creek is dry, but water does flow through it after heavy rains. At the bottom of this hill the trail crosses a large creek bed near a downed tree. The trail on the other side can be difficult to find—it's off to the left.

The River View Trail connects with several other trails in this part of the Wayne National Forest. Archer's Fork is the closest such trail, but it can be difficult to reach. It may not look very far away on a map, but the challenging terrain—including thick woods that require frequent portages over downed trees—can turn the link-up into an all-day epic.

Bicycle Camping

I f you consider your mountain bike saddle the most comfortable seat in the house and crave an opportunity to prove your self-sufficiency, try bicycle camping. It does require more planning and preparation than a standard day trip, but the particular satisfaction gained from reaching a campground or a remote outdoor destination on two wheels, knowing you're ready for a cozy night outdoors, makes the extra effort worthwhile.

If you plan on doing a lot of bicycle camping/touring, it's a good idea to invest in quality equipment. Everyone should have a pair of medium-to-large size panniers that can be mounted on a rear rack (if you are planning a long trip, you might consider a front rack). A lightweight backpacking tent, sleeping pad, and sleeping bag can be attached to the rear rack using two or three bungie cords. We all have a tendency to over-pack, but the extra weight of unnecessary equipment may cause you to tire more easily. Here are some tips to help you find the appropriate amount of gear:

- Bring a multi-purpose tool that has a can opener, bottle opener, scissors, knife, and screwdriver.
- Pack only one extra change of clothes, plus any necessary layers such as a polypropylene shirt and tights, polar fleece, wool socks, and rain gear. If you are on a multi-day trip, bring extra shorts and t-shirts, and if it's winter, bring an extra pair of polypropylene tights and shirt, as well as a few extra pairs of wool socks.
- Bring a tin cup and spoon for eating and drinking and one lightweight pot for cooking.
- Invest in a lightweight backpacking stove, tent, and sleeping bag.
- Bring along freeze dried food. You can buy many pre-packaged rice and noodle mixes in the grocery store for half of what you'll pay at backpacking stores.
- Bring the minimum amount of water needed for your intended route. Anticipate if there will be water available. Invest in a water filter that can be used to filter water from water sources along the trail.

Equipment List

Use the checklist of equipment below when you are planning for a single or multi-day trip. You can develop your own equipment list based on the length of your trip, the time of year, weather conditions, and difficulty of the trail.

Essentials
- bungie cords
- compass
- day panniers
- duct tape
- fenders
- pocket knife or multi-purpose tool
- rear rack
- front rack
- trail map
- water bottles
- water filter
- tool kit
- patch kit
- crescent wrench
- tire levers
- spoke wrench
- extra spokes
- chain rivet tool
- extra tube
- tire pump

Clothing
- rain jacket/pants
- polar fleece jacket
- wool sweater
- helmet liner
- bicycle tights
- t-shirts/shorts
- sturdy bicycle shoes/boots
- swimsuit
- underwear
- bike gloves
- eye protection
- bike helmet/liner

First Aid Kit
- bandages (various sizes)
- gauze pads
- surgical tape
- antibiotic ointment
- hydrogen peroxide or iodine
- gauze roll
- ace bandage
- aspirin
- moleskin
- sunscreen
- insect repellent

Personal Items
- towel
- toothbrush/toothpaste
- soap
- comb
- shampoo

Camping Items
- backpacking stove
- tent
- sleeping bag
- foam pad
- cooking and eating utensils
- can opener
- flashlight/batteries
- candle lantern
- touring panniers
- pannier rain covers
- zip-lock bags
- large heavy duty plastic garbage bags
- citronella candles (to repel insects)
- small duffels to organize gear

Miscellaneous Items
- camera/film/batteries
- notebook/pen
- paperback book

Tip:
Zip-lock bags are a great way to waterproof and organize your gear. Large, heavy-duty plastic garbage bags also make excellent waterproof liners for the inside of your panniers.

Covered Bridge Trail

Ride Summary

The Marietta Unit of the Wayne National Forest is one of the most isolated and wild areas of Ohio, a fact that may explain why it remains relatively undiscovered by mountain bikers. But singletrack junkies who brave the lengthy drive to this area will be treated to some of the longest stretches of singletrack in the state. The Covered Bridge Trail—with its challenging climbs, gentle singletrack, technical rocky sections, and big descents—is a blast to ride.

Ride Specs

Start: Haught Run Campground on OH 26
Length: 8.2-mile out-and-back
Approximate Riding Time: 1–1½ hours
Difficulty Rating: Technically difficult due to rocky creek crossings, steep climbs and descents, and tight switchbacks
Trail Surface: Singletrack and gravel roads
Lay of the Land: Wooded and rocky
Elevation Gain: 403 feet
Land Status: National forest
Nearest Town: Marietta
Other Trail Users: Hunters and hikers

Getting There

From Marietta: Take OH 26 east about 15 miles to a turnoff for the Haught Run Recreation Area. The trail begins at the camping area about one mile from OH 26. *DeLorme: Ohio Atlas & Gazetteer.* Page 72, D-1

This trail takes its name from the two covered bridges that span the Little Muskingum River at the beginning and end of the ride. The beginning of the ride—in the narrow valley of the Haught Run Campground—is similar to the bridges: flat and covered with a canopy of wood. After a muddy creek crossing, this flat section of trail parallels Haught Run for a while. There are a couple of technical, rocky creek crossings here, but don't worry about getting soaked—the water is rarely more than a couple of inches deep.

When the trail finally veers away from the creek it climbs up the steep hill in a series of switchbacks. Resign yourself to pushing here, because this section is almost impossible to clean. Thankfully, it's not very long.

Once on top of the hill, the trail is a roller-coaster singletrack. It winds through the trees and has only minor elevation changes. The tacky soil lends confidence to riders who like to take singletrack turns at high speeds.

Before there were cars, there were bikes and covered bridges.

And the speed only picks up as the trail turns downhill. There are a couple of tricky descents heading down to the covered bridge at the end of the ride, but for the most part the trail is open and very fast. The gravel road will take you back to the singletrack at the top of the hill, but it's more fun to ride back up the trail.

The majority of the covered bridges in Ohio lie in Washington County, home to Marietta and the Marietta district of the Wayne National Forest. Ohio's legacy of covered bridges began when white settlers came to Ohio from New England after the Revolutionary War. Wood was used to build the bridges because it was cheaper than iron or stone. Technological advances also made the use of wood practical. Truss systems, with interlocking triangles of timber, allowed great spans to support heavy loads.

MilesDirections

0.0 START at the Haught Run Campground, cross the creek, and hit the trail to the left.

0.6 Climb to the left of the creek.

0.8 Cross the creek, but continue to ride parallel to it, then cross it again to the other side of a ravine.

0.9 The trail switchbacks several times on its way to the top of the ridge.

1.1 After a steep climb, reach the top of the ridge.

1.5 Go straight across T 35.

2.3 Go straight across T 34 to the Covered Bridge Trail.

2.7 Go around the point of the ridge; the gravel road is off to the left.

2.8 Turn right at T 34 then quickly turn left onto the singletrack.

3.1 Turn right into a stand of pine trees.

3.7 Cross under the power line.

3.9 After a downhill along a gully, hit T 34 and turn right.

4.2 Turn around at the Hune Covered Bridge and double back to the start.

8.4 Reach the end the ride back at the Haught Run Campground.

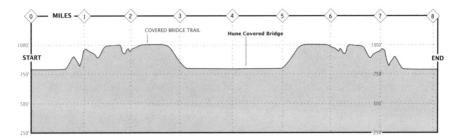

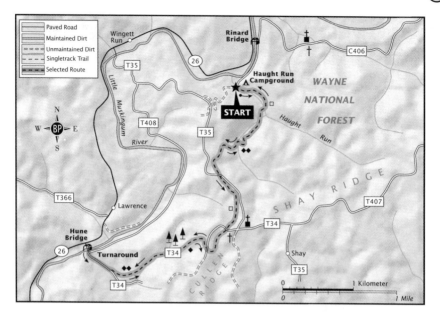

steep hills + mud = stuck in BFE

Ride Information

Trail Contacts:
Ohio Historic Bridge Association
3155 Whitehead Road
Columbus, OH

Wayne National Forest
Athens, OH
(614) 592-6644

Schedule:
April 15 to November 15

Local Information:
Marietta/Washington County
Convention and Visitors Bureau
Marietta, OH
1-888-659-7968

Accommodations:
Wayne National Forest
(primitive camping)
Athens, OH
(614) 592-6644

Maps:
USGS map: Rinard Mills, OH; Dalzell, OH

Covered Bridge Wishes

Want to make sure a covered-bridge wish comes true? Make a wish before crossing a covered bridge, lift your feet off the floor of your vehicle, take a deep breath, and say, "bunny, bunny, bunny, bunny..." all the way across the bridge while thinking of your wish. When on the other side, say "Rabbit!" Try it and let us know if your wish comes true!

There are many guesses as to why the bridges are covered. Some say the roofs keep the snow off. Others say the bridges were built to resemble barns to make horses comfortable. Some believe the builders covered the bridges to keep the taxpayers from seeing the shoddy workmanship under the wooden shell. Still others feel that the bridges were designed to protect travelers caught in storms.

But the hard fact is that wooden bridges survive much longer when covered. The wooden trusses holding the bridges together would rot in about 10 years if they weren't protected. When covered, their life span increases to nearly 100 years. Monetary considerations also came into play—the first covered bridges were also toll bridges.

It's estimated that between 400 and 500 covered bridges once existed in Ohio. Because the bridges were often the largest covered areas in a community, they were often used for public gatherings. Ministers would hold revivals under the cover of the bridges and politicians would hold political rallies. Couples would even use the bridges for their marriage ceremonies. Today, due to increased traffic, heavier loads, fire, and floods, only about 125 such bridges remain.

Honorable Mentions

Southeast Ohio

Compiled here is an index of great rides in Southeast Ohio that didn't make the A-list this time around but deserve recognition. Check them out and let us know what you think. You may decide that one or more of these rides deserves higher status in future editions or, perhaps, you may have a ride of your own that merits some attention.

Ⓓ Richland Furnace

Southern Ohio is full of the remains of industry from the turn of the century. In the case of Richland Furnace State Forest, the ruin is an old furnace once used to smelt iron. The ORV trails of Richland Furnace closely resemble those of Monday Creek. There are lots of fast descents and arduous climbs on this nine-mile trail system. But unlike Monday Creek, there is only one way in and out. Because of its location, these trails see less ORV traffic than other areas in Southern Ohio. The trails have fewer ruts than more heavily used areas, but the industrial legacy of the area is still visible. It was recently clearcut in places, so call ahead for trail conditions if you find yourself in this neck of the woods.

From Chillicothe, take U.S. Route 50 East to Ohio 327 South. Turn right on Ohio 327 and follow southeast about 10 miles to Loop Road. Turn left onto Loop Road and follow to the Richland Furnace ORV trailhead on the left. Call (614) 593-3341 for trail information. *DeLorme: Ohio Atlas & Gazetteer:* Page 79, 5-C

Ⓔ Main Corridor

At more than 20 miles, the Main Corridor Trail is the longest trail in the Monday Creek Off-Road Vehicle Area. The trail begins in New Straightsville, follows part of Snake Hollow and then goes to Dorr Run. Like other trails in Monday Creek, the climbs are long and the downhills are fast. But there are also some long flat areas and some fun rock formations to play on. If you want to ride the whole thing, shuttle a car to one end of the trail because riding the whole thing out and back is very difficult. From Athens, head north on U.S. Route 33. Exit at Ohio 595 and turn right. The New Straightsville trailhead is about seven miles on the right. For more information call the Athens Ranger District at (740) 592-6644. *DeLorme: Ohio Atlas & Gazetteer:* Page 70, D-1

Ⓕ Dorr Run

The most popular trail in Monday Creek, Dorr Run is where most mountain bikers get their first taste of the Wayne National Forest—and subsequently get lost. There are a lot of trails here, many not marked or accessed by the main 16-mile loop. Forest service maps don't help much. The main loop is an awesome ride, with some very fast riding—expert riders do the loop in about 1.25 hours. Mere mortals can spend three hours. Beware of heavy ORV traffic on the weekends.

From Nelsonville take U.S. Route 33 north about 10 miles then turn right on Township 336 (there is a small trailhead sign—you'll know you've passed it if the highway turns into four lanes). Begin the ride from the first parking area. The trail is about 200 yards farther up the road on the right. For more information call the Athens Ranger District at (740) 592-6644. *DeLorme: Ohio Atlas & Gazetteer:* Page 79, A-7

(G) Purdum Trail

The Purdum Trail is a spur of the Dorr Run Loop. The out-and-back ride has one of the longest descents in the Wayne National Forest—but you also have to climb it. There are some fun rock sections in the beginning.

From the beginning of the Dorr Run ride, head about 300 yards up the road and jump on the Dorr Run Trail to the left. At the top of the climb, the Purdum Trail splits off to the left. At the gravel road go straight across. For more information call the Athens Ranger District at (740) 592-6644. *DeLorme: Ohio Atlas & Gazetteer:* Page 79, A-7

(H) Lake Hope State Park

So far, the only trail sanctioned for mountain biking at Lake Hope State Park is the two-mile Little Sandy Trail. But with the help of the Ohio University Mountain Bike Club, the park service is investigating putting in a trail around the lake, which could total 10 miles. The Little Sandy Trail begins and ends on Cabin Ridge Road and offers a bit of climbing and some nice views of Lake Hope.

From Athens, take Ohio 56 East to Ohio 278. Head south on Ohio 278 then turn right on Cabin Ridge Road, past the park office. For information call Lake Hope State Park at (614) 596-5253. *DeLorme: Ohio Atlas & Gazetteer:* Page 79, B-7

(I) Kanawha State Forest, West Virginia

This is the place get your fix for some truly technical singletrack. A fire road climb delivers you to all the trails, which then head down—some very steeply. The Black Bear and Pine Tree trails are some of the best.

From Marietta take Interstate 77 South to Charleston, West Virginia, to Interstate 64 East. In Charleston take the Oakwood Road exit onto U.S. Route 119 South. At the second light turn left. Signs for park start once on Oakwood Road. At the bottom of a large hill, take a sharp left. This road goes to the park. For information call (304) 558-3500. *DeLorme: West Virginia Atlas & Gazetteer:* Page 52, A-2

(J) Archer's Fork

Though this trail is very remote, it has some great terrain. Along its 9.5 miles there are many excellent downhills and technical climbs. There is also a natural bridge—one of only seven in Ohio. This loop can be combined with the Covered Bridge and Scenic River trails for a true epic.

From Marietta take Ohio 7 north to New Matamoros. Turn left in New Matamoros onto Ohio 260. Turn left on Township 14 for the closest trailhead. The roads are muddy when it rains and can be impassable in places. For more information call the Marietta Ranger District at (740) 373-9055. *DeLorme: Ohio Atlas & Gazetteer:* Page 72, D-3

(K) Lamping Homestead

The Lamping Homestead trails are similar to other trails in the Marietta District of the Wayne National Forest. There are strenuous climbs and nice downhills, with some great singletrack in between. There are five miles of trails here.

From Marietta take Ohio 26 east. Turn left on Ohio 537. The Lamping Homestead Trail will be on your left. For more information call the Marietta Ranger District at (740) 373-9055. *DeLorme: Ohio Atlas & Gazetteer:* Page 72, C-2

Northeast

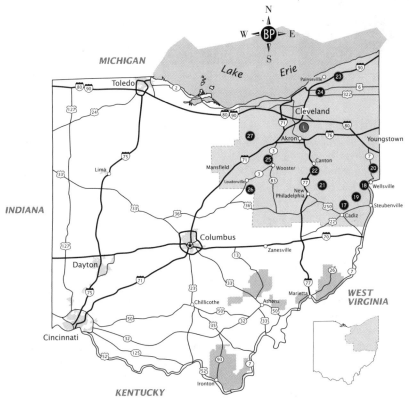

N

ortheast Ohio is a mixture of urban sprawl and rural landscapes. Most of the land in and around Akron, Canton,
or Cleveland is fully developed. That, coupled with a
shortage of urban parks, tends to force the mountain bike
community into the countryside, where they can find
numerous riding opportunities. These range from the
mild Findlay State Park to the downright gnarly Wellsville.

The majority of the rides in the region take full advantage of the rolling
hills, steep river valleys, and wooded terrain. The trails in Vulture's Knob
utilize every available obstacle. The area is littered with steep climbs, log
crossings, and crazy log bridges.

Northeast Ohio has some of the best race series in the state. Alpine
Valley, Mohican, Mickey's Mountain, and Vulture's Knob all hold at least
one race a month during the season. All of the courses are challenging and
fun and attract a wide range of riders from moderate skill levels to top cal-
iber downhill and dual slalom riders. Though some of these rides are in very
rural, far away locations, none are more than a couple of hours from
Cleveland. Riders in Akron and Canton will have even less to drive for
most of the rides.

Mickey's Mountain

Ride Summary

Because it's a racecourse, the trail at Mickey's Mountain is very fast. But it's also quite technical in places. There are more than 1,700 feet of climbing per lap and many of those climbs are extremely steep. The downhills range from fast and smooth to precipitous, bumpy, and off-camber. Throw in a few creek crossings for good measure and the course becomes an exceptional challenge. There are three race loops from which to choose and the courses are always changing. Make sure you call ahead for permission if you're planning to ride on a non-race day. All of the courses begin from the barn at the top of the hill.

Ride Specs

Start: The barn at the top of Ford Road
Length: 5 miles per loop
Approximate Riding Time: 1 hour
Difficulty Rating: Technically difficult due to the tricky singletrack climbs and descents
Trail Surface: Singletrack, doubletrack, and dirt access roads
Lay of the Land: Twisty singletrack and short climbs and descents with off-camber sections
Land Status: Private
Nearest Town: Hopedale
Other Trail Users: Hay farmers

Getting There

From New Philadelphia: Follow U.S. 250 east to U.S. 22. Take U.S. 22 east to Miller Station Road and turn left (north). Follow Miller Station Road 3.5 miles and turn left onto County Road 46 after the railroad tracks. Continue for half a mile and turn right on Ford Road just before a green house. Park at the top of the hill in the field. *DeLorme: Ohio Atlas & Gazetteer.* Page 63, B-5

Hard-working Calvin Mickey is the James Brown of Ohio mountain biking. But unlike James Brown, Calvin does not seek fame or fortune in his pursuits. He is motivated only by a need to put on the finest racing series in the state.

Mickey's Mountain Bike Challenge began in 1994 when Calvin's son began riding mountain bikes. At the time, there were few big races in the state that could deliver a professional atmosphere and a course to match. So with more than 350 acres of terrain with which to play, Calvin set about making one of the most challenging courses in Ohio. That same year he hosted the NORBA state championships.

With lots of effort, Mickey's Mountain Bike Challenge has become the premier off-road racing series in Ohio. What began as a five-mile course has evolved into 15 miles of trails and separate courses for beginners and juniors. The sport/expert course has about 1,700 feet of climbing per lap, which, as Calvin points out, is equivalent to many of the NORBA national courses. And the course is different every month so racers never get bored.

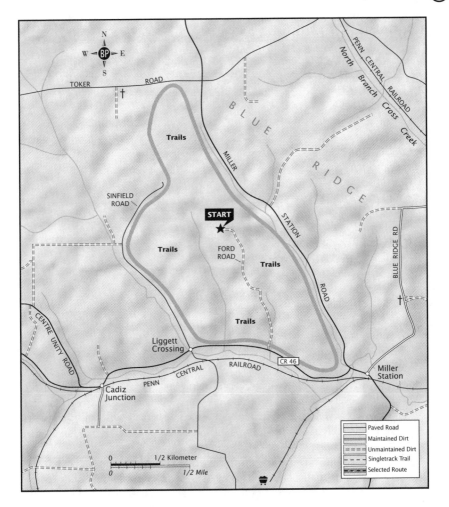

MilesDirections

No directions can be given for this ride as the course is always changing. The course markings for each race remain up until they are changed for the next race, so use these as a guide. The expert course is recommended as the most fun and challenging ride. All the loops begin at the barn and are clearly marked when they split from the expert loop.

Ride Information

Trail Contacts:
Calvin and Kathy Mickey
Hopedale, OH
(740) 946-5631
www.mickeysmtn.com

Schedule:
Open year-round

Fees/Permits:
$5 per rider per day

Local Information:
Harrison Regional Chamber of
Commerce
Cadiz, OH
(740) 942-3350

Local Events/Attractions:
Mickey's Mountain Racing
www.mickeysmtn.com

Accommodations:
Primitive camping is allowed on the
property for $5 per day. Call ahead
for permission.

Maps:
USGS map: Cadiz, OH

Calvin takes racer input very seriously and constantly makes changes to keep everyone happy. When riders wanted a slalom course Calvin built one. When advanced riders said they wanted a slalom course with jumps and berms, Calvin built that, too. Now riders can pick a course to match their skill level.

Trials riders can also get their fix at Mickey's Mountain. Calvin has built a series of trial courses to challenge riders of every ability. Cars, boulders, logs, and other debris litter the courses. There is even a chain-link swing to wow riders and spectators alike.

When the gravity set demanded a downhill course, Calvin brought out the chainsaw and cut a challenging 1,400-foot descent through the woods. He wrapped trees with hay bales and foam to protect them and riddled one section with rocks to add to the challenge. He further pampered riders by building a new road so he could haul them back to the start after a race. And he invested in timing equipment that rivals those at the best ski resorts in the nation.

Hundreds of riders show up for the races each month. On average, more than 350 competitors enter each event. In 1998 riders from 30 states competed, as did riders from Ireland, Africa, Wales, and Italy. Part of keeping all these racers happy is giving them money, prizes, and quick race results. Calvin dished out over $40,000 in door prizes in 1998 and paid $25,000 in cash to those who placed. And results are posted as soon as a racer crosses the finish line.

But Mickey's Mountain is not all about racing. The course is a great place for spectators; those who don't want to hike into the woods can watch the slalom or trials competitions. There is also a race for kids. And trail riders who want to bike the course on non-race days can do so any time—just follow Calvin's rules. That's the least you can do in return for all his hard work.

Mr. Mickey has thrown in some very steep climbs.

141

Wellsville

Ride Summary

If you're looking for technical riding in Ohio you'll find it in Wellsville. The town's trail system was originally developed by off-road and power-company vehicles. The climbs are definitely challenging—probably the hardest of all the rides covered in this book. But each climb is rewarded with a very long, and often very technical, downhill. The trails are not marked and crisscross the steep hills of the area, so it's easy to get lost. Bring a compass, lots of water, and a friend. If you do find yourself disoriented, remember that the Ohio River is to the east and Yellow Creek is to the south.

Ride Specs

Start: From the gravel access road just after the railroad tracks south of Wellsville

Length: Routes of varying distances are possible.

Approximate Riding Time: 1–4 hours

Difficulty Rating: Difficult due to long, steep climbs and rocky descents

Trail Surface: Doubletrack ORV trails, singletrack, and gravel roads

Lay of the Land: Very hilly and rocky

Land Status: Public

Nearest Town: Wellsville

Other Trail Users: Off-road vehicles and hunters

Getting There

From Wellsville: Head south on OH 7. Turn left (west) on 21st Street by the old foundry at the "Welcome to Wellsville" sign. Continue on 21st Street for about two miles as it follows Yellow Creek. You'll come to a house on the right and, immediately after it, a gravel road. Turn right here, cross the railroad tracks, and park.

DeLorme: Ohio Atlas & Gazetteer: Page 53, D-6

J ust south of the town of Wellsville, Ohio, lies one of the most technical and extreme rides in the state. Everything from massive hills to sharp rocks beckon even the most skilled mountain bikers to spill a little blood.

The first human to shed blood on this land was not too far from where this ride begins, on the Ohio River at the mouth of Yellow Creek. In the spring of 1774 rumors circulated up and down the Ohio River that Native Americans were on the warpath killing every white person they came across. These rumors turned out to be nothing more than blatant lies, serving only to turn white settlers against the natives. When one settler, Jacob Greathouse, heard that a party of Shawnee (they were actually Mingo tribesmen, led by Talgayeeta) was at Yellow Creek, he rounded up about 30 men for an attack.

The event that ensued would make any man cringe. Greathouse and a few of his men went to the Mingo village at Yellow Creek, offered the natives a keg of whiskey, and challenged them to a contest of marksmanship. The Mingos were fond of both liquor and gambling, and a group of about 10 men and women accepted the settlers' challenge. They went to a site on the mouth of Yellow Creek where the Mingo insisted that Greathouse and his men shoot first. Of the seven that shot, about three or four hit the target. Then it was the Mingos' turn. But as they lined up to shoot, the rest of Greathouse's posse jumped from the bushes and killed the Mingo men. The only survivors were the women-Talgayeeta's sister,

Mellana, and his wife, Koonay. Both were scalped and killed soon thereafter by Greathouse's posse. This incident spurred Lord Dunmore's War in 1774.

More than 200 years later, cyclists are now on the warpath here at Wellsville and Yellow Creek. And while helmets may prevent cyclists from getting scalped on the Wellsville trails, an errant rock or root may conspire to at least separate you from your bike. Some of the downhills are hideously technical, littered with large rocks and drop-offs. Skilled riders should be able to negotiate most of them, but a few are better traversed on foot. But not all of the descents are so treacherous. Some are simply fast doubletrack trails created by off-road vehicles brought back here for maintenance on the power lines.

Like most off-road vehicle trails in Ohio, those at Wellsville have their fair share of jumps. Some of the best are at the beginning of the ride at the top of the hill. The area has a large bowl that safely rockets riders down and then up its steep slopes. It's almost like a half-pipe for mountain bikers.

The climbs are steep-thanks to the fact that ORVs tend to drive straight up hills-but generally smooth. But the suffering required to ascend these massive hills is worth the views (to the east are the Ohio River and West Virginia; to the west is the rest of Ohio) and the fast return trips downhill.

MilesDirections

Begin the Wellsville ride from the gravel road just past the railroad tracks. Follow the road to the top of the hill and jump on the trails from there. Because of the nature of the Wellsville trail system, it's unreasonable to try to follow a single loop. You'll find a maze of trails that are difficult to ride in all directions. Be pre-pared to encounter technical downhills and steep climbs and hike-a-bikes. Orienteering skills are a must here, as accurate trail maps are impossible to come by (and impossible to make). Allow plenty of time for this ride, as a 10-mile loop may take as long as three or four hours; and bring plenty of food and water.

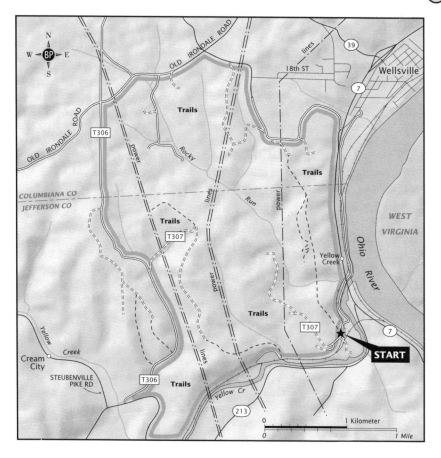

Ride Information

Trail Contacts:
Ernie's Bike Shop
Massillon, OH
(330) 832-5111

Schedule:
Open year-round; trails should be avoided when muddy

Accommodations:
Lake Cha-Vel-Painted Post
Wellsville, OH (330) 532-4828

Local Information:
Columbiana County Convention and Visitors Bureau
Lisbon, OH
(330) 424-9078

Maps:
USGS map: Wellsville, OH

Jefferson Lake State Park

Ride Summary

Most of the trails at Jefferson Lake State Park are multiple-use and probably see more horses than bikers. The wider bridle trails are sometimes muddy in the low sections but are in pretty good shape overall. The riding is not very technical but, with the steep climbs and long, fast downhills, is still fun and challenging. The Downhill Trail is the most technical of the paths and is a perfect way to finish a ride. There's a shaded picnic area at its end, and the beach and swimming area are nearby.

Ride Specs

Start: Campground registration station at Jefferson Lake State Park
Length: 3.7 miles
Approximate Riding Time: 45 minutes
Difficulty Rating: Intermediate due to the steep climbs and muddy trails
Trail Surface: Mostly bridle trails and singletrack; some road riding
Elevation Gain: -165 feet
Land Status: State park
Nearest Town: Wintersville
Other Trail Users: Equestrians and hikers

Getting There

From Steubenville: Take OH 22 west, then turn right on OH 43 in Wintersville. After about nine miles, turn right on CR 53. Continue past Jefferson Lake (on the left), then turn left at the Jefferson Lake State Park entrance. Park at the camper registration area and start the ride on the trail to the right. *DeLorme: Ohio Atlas & Gazetteer.* Page 63, A-5

Though Jefferson Lake State Park is just around the corner from Wellsville, the two areas couldn't be more different when it comes to their mountain biking trails. The Wellsville trails are extreme in all directions because of the steep and rocky terrain that has been chewed up by dirt bikes and four-wheel-drive vehicles. On the other hand, the trails at Jefferson Lake State Park, while extreme in places, have seen no motorized traffic and are therefore less eroded. There are no rocks or cavernous ruts conspiring to detach riders from their bikes. The forest here is also thicker and more natural than that at Wellsville. A second growth forest of towering white oaks and shagbark hickories grow side-by-side here with stately beeches and maples, tulip trees, walnuts, elms and ashes. One thing the Jefferson Lake State Park does have in common with the Wellsville area is its shared history with the Mingo Indians. The Jefferson Lake region was once home to Logan, the Mingo chief whose family was massacred by Jacob Greathouse and his posse at the mouth of Yellow Creek in 1774.

It gets hot and muggy in the summer.

Few of the trails at Jefferson Lake State Park are singletrack. Most of the trails were carved into the woods using brush hogs and bulldozers and are very wide—a good thing when you're bombing down steep hills through sharp turns. In some places, however, there is still old vegetation, making climbing and cornering difficult. In other places the bulldozers simply cut the trails straight up and down the hills. This may be fine for a horse, but it spells frustration for cyclists attempting to pedal the steep grades.

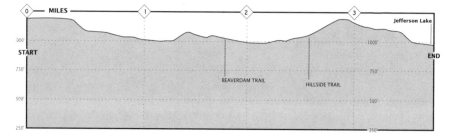

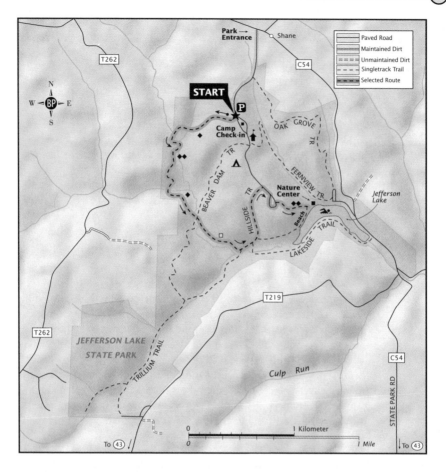

MilesDirections

0.0 START at the camper registration area. The trailhead is to the right of the parking lot.

0.3 Cross the creek then go uphill.

0.8 Cross the creek at the bottom of the hill.

0.9 Cross another creek.

1.3 Traverse a muddy hike-a-bike section after the creek.

1.7 Turn right onto the Beaver Dam Trail.

2.4 Continue straight on the Beaver Dam Trail. The Trillium Trail is to the right.

2.5 Go straight. The Lakeside Trail is to the right.

2.6 Go left up the Hillside Trail.

3.0 At the top of the Hillside Trail go straight through the playground.

3.0 Turn right at the road and then right again at the turn-off for the campground.

3.2 Follow the one-way road to the right.

3.4 Follow the Downhill Trail to the right.

3.7 Finish the ride with a soak at the beach. Return to the camper registration area along one of the many routes on the map.

Ride Information

Trail Contacts:
Jefferson Lake State Park
Richmond, OH
(740) 765-4459

Schedule:
Open year-round

Other Resources:
Ohio Parks and Tourism Directory;
www.ohioparks.net/jeffersonlake

Accommodations:
Jefferson Lake State Park
(camping)
Richmond, OH
(740) 765-4459

**Greater Steubenville Convention
and Visitor's Bureau**
Steubenville, OH
1-800-510-4442

Maps:
USGS map: Richmond, OH

Horses extensively use many of these trails, especially those away from the lake and parking area. As always, mountain bikers should yield to horses in all situations. In fact, when it's wet it's a good idea to avoid the horse trails altogether. The soil here is soft and horses tend to leave deep craters which, when wet, turn to huge mud holes.

Even if it hasn't rained recently, some of the trails can still be muddy. Trillium, Beaver Dam, Lakeside, and Logan's Trails all follow creeks and lowlands at certain points and remain muddy for quite a while after it rains. They also see a fair amount of horse traffic, which doesn't help trail conditions.

The Oak Grove, Fernview, Downhill and Hillside Trails are the least used by horses. And because they're older and more established, they are also narrower than the trails on the outer reaches of the park. The aptly named Downhill Trail is steep and technical in places and can only be ridden going downhill. Oak Grove, Fernview, and Hillside, on the other hand, have steep sections, but can all be ridden in either direction, up or down.

The Beaver Dam Trail has some very fun sections with fast descents and gentle climbs. The beaver dam itself is hard to see through the trees, but is off to the west of the trail on one of the trail's flat points. Don't count on seeing any beaver, though—this shy and elusive animal is rarely seen outside of the Discovery Channel.

Several loops can be taken in addition to the one described below. A good long loop starts at the check-in station: Take Logan's Trail south to the trailhead on Township Road 219, head north on the Trillium Trail, turn right on the Beaver Dam Trail, then return to the check-in station on Oak Grove Trail. The roads surrounding the park can also be used to make loops.

If you choose not to end your ride at the beach (as per the recommended ride in this book), the Fernview Trail will take you back up the hill to the check-in station. Alternatively, you can ride back up the road to the start.

Jefferson Lake State Park is a great place to camp. Several of the park's campsites offer views of the lake in the valley below. The park also can serve as a central base camp to several other good mountain biking areas nearby, including Mickey's Mountain, Wellsville, and Beaver Creek State Park.

The picnic table won this battle.

Beaver Creek State Park

Ride Summary

The dramatic landscape of this area in Eastern Ohio makes for both good scenery and good riding. The trails of Beaver Creek State Park follow the contours of the valley, from the creek to the ridges above it. There is a good mix of trails here. The ride begins with an easy cruise and gets increasingly more difficult as the ride progresses up and down the hills. Steep climbs and rocky descents add a nice technical touch.

Ride Specs

Start: From the Beaver Creek State Park Pioneer Village
Length: 12.3-mile
Approximate Riding Time: 2 hours
Difficulty Rating: Moderate-difficult due to rocky trails and long climbs
Trail Surface: Singletrack
Lay of the Land: Wooded, rocky valley overlooking Beaver Creek
Elevation Gain (Loop A): 860 feet
Elevation Gain (Loop B): 1,366 feet
Land Status: State park
Nearest Town: East Liverpool
Other Trail Users: Hikers and hunters (in season)

Getting There

From East Liverpool: Take OH 7 north and turn right on Bell School Road (look for the school) Turn left at Echo Dell Road and follow to the Pioneer Village. Park here. ***DeLorme: Ohio Atlas & Gazetteer.*** Page 53 C-7

A bove Little Beaver Creek in Columbiana County, Ohio, the quiet sound of wind through the trees barely mutes the rushing waters nearly 500 feet below. To say that the view from this point—Sprucevale Overlook—is one of the finest in the state just doesn't do it justice. Only after a day of pedaling up and down the gorge, sweating and covered with bits of mud and maybe a wound or two, can the rewards of this view truly be appreciated. As the setting sun casts its golden light upon the valley, the reward is something that may not be attained anywhere else, and the soul is full until darkness casts its shadow.

Just across the gorge from the Sprucevale Overlook lies Beaver Creek State Park. This 3,038-acre wilderness haven is home to several different habitats including bottomlands, a sandstone gorge, deep forests, and Little Beaver Creek. Stretches of the creek were designated a Wild and Scenic

Beaver Creek.

River by the state in 1974, and a year later 33 miles of the creek were designated a National Scenic River—including the portion that flows through the park. In addition to its human visitors, the park boasts an array of wildlife including red fox, skunk, raccoon, and white-tailed deer. Wild turkey are making a comeback, and even black bear have been sighted.

153

MilesDirections

Loop A

0.0 START at the parking lot at the bottom of the hill and ride north across bridge.

0.1 Turn left on the Creek Trail.

0.3 Go left on the road.

0.5 Enter the Dogwood Trail at end of road along creek.

1.8 The Dogwood Trail switchbacks up the hill.

2.9 Turn left to go to the Pine Ridge Trail.

3.1 Go left at the road. Go right at next two road intersections.

3.3 Turn left to the Pine Ridge Trail.

3.6 Take the left fork in the trail.

4.0 Turn right on the road.

4.1 Turn left on the first road, then left again (you are retracing your steps).

4.2 Turn right back to the Dogwood Trail.

4.4 Turn left on the Dogwood Trail.

4.6 Stay left on top of the ridge.

4.7 Turn left following the road to the bridge.

Loop B

4.8 Turn left just before the bridge on a small trail following the creek.

5.6 After a bridge crossing, go right following the Vondergreen Trail signs.

6.0 Follow the right fork, staying on the Vondergreen Trail.

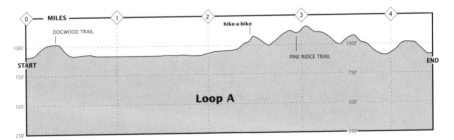

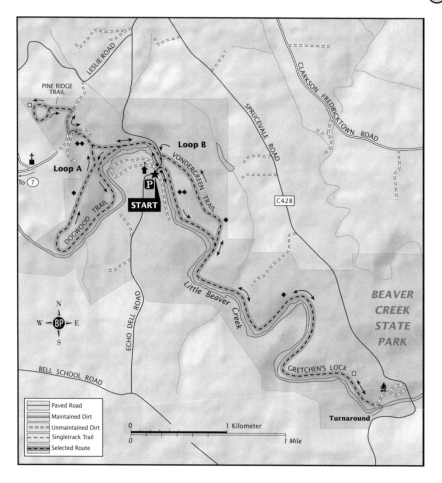

6.4 Turn left by Gretchen's Lock.
6.5 Turn left after bridge and up the hill.
6.6 Follow Vondergreen Trail to right.
7.7 Turn left before Gretchen's Lock sign.
8.4 Turn around at the camping area.
10.6 At bottom of hill go right at bridge.
10.7 Turn right at the lock.

11.5 Follow the Vondergreen Trail right up hill.
11.8 Turn right following the "No horses" sign.
12.1 Turn left.
12.2 Turn left down hill.
12.4 Turn left at the road.
12.7 End ride at parking lot.

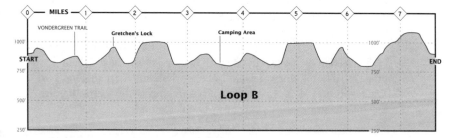

Ride Information

Trail Contacts:
Beaver Creek State Park
East Liverpool, OH
(330) 385-3091

Schedule:
Open year-round

Local Information:
Beaver Creek State Park
East Liverpool, OH
(330) 385-3091

Columbiana County Visitors Bureau
East Liverpool, OH
(330) 424-9078

Local Events/Attractions:
Pioneer Craft Days
Oct 5 and 6
East Liverpool, OH
(330) 385-3091

Maps:
USGS maps: East Liverpool North, OH; Westpoint, OH

Mountain bikers probably won't see any deer, but the park's scenery and excellent trails will make up for this. The 15-mile hiking trail system is open to bikes. A good place to start the ride is on the Dogwood Trail following the river. The trail starts off flat and is decidedly easy for a good stretch, allowing for a decent warm-up. The trail climbs soon enough and gives riders a taste of some technical rock riding. From the Dogwood Trail, riders can make the difficult jaunt to the campground and the fast, rooty Pine Ridge Trail. The return ride from Pine Ridge to the beginning of Dogwood is very rocky and rewards technically proficient riders.

Not far from the Dogwood Trail is the Vondergreen Trail. The trail actually begins just down from the bridge, but beginning right at the bridge gives riders a chance to practice their trials skills and avoid a big climb. The Vondergreen Trail passes the remnants of several canal locks and a gristmill. Ninety locks and 30 dams were built in the area in 1834 to connect to the Ohio and Erie Canal. Hopes of commercial success for the project were quickly dashed with the coming of the railroad a few years later, and the canal project was abandoned.

Riders pass Gretchen's Lock as they pedal along the Vondergreen Trail. The lock is said to contain the tomb of the engineer's daughter, Gretchen Gill. Shortly after arriving in Ohio, the engineer's daughter Gretchen died and the heartbroken father buried her in a vault in the lock on which he was working.

Ride quickly, if not to avoid Gretchen's ghost, then to enjoy the fast trails on this section of the trail. Every climb is rewarded with an excellent downhill. Probably the finest downhill of the whole ride is at the end of the Vondergreen Trail. It is a bit bumpy, but the higher the speed, the higher the enjoyment factor—a perfect way to end the ride.

Along the Vondergreen Trail riders will notice the many equestrian trails. There are over 23 miles of trail designated for horseback riding, but it is best to stay off of these to avoid the inevitable "landmine." Park officials also prefer that cyclists stick to the hiking trails. If you have an inclination to ride the rapids, Little Beaver Creek offers one of the most exciting canoe trips in the state.

Those looking to make a weekend trip of riding should consider using the Beaver Creek campgrounds as a homebase. The campsites are some of the best in the state and the location is central to many other rides in the area including Wellsville, Jefferson Lake State Park, and Mickey's Mountain in Hopedale.

Atwood Lake Park

Ride Summary

For the most part, the trails that make up this ride at Atwood are very easy to navigate. They form two rough circles on a ridge overlooking the lake and are well marked. Other than the long initial climb and a couple of other short, steep hills, the trails are not very technical. Rather, they're fairly wide and have only a few rocks. Accordingly, speeds are high on the downhills and on the flats. At the end of the ride, cruise down to the beach for a cool dip in the lake.

Ride Specs

Start: Trail sign below the fire tower
Length: 3.9-mile loop
Approximate Riding Time: 1 hour
Difficulty Rating: Technically easy to moderate due to the long climb and fast trails
Trail Surface: Doubletrack, singletrack, and gravel roads
Lay of the Land: Hilly
Elevation Gain: 276 feet
Land Status: Regional Park
Nearest Town: Carrollton
Other Trail Users: Hikers

Getting There

From Canton: Drive south on I-77 to OH 212. Follow OH 212 east to Atwood Lake Road. Turn left (east) on Atwood Lake Road and park at the marina. Pedal your bike into the park if you want to save $4 in your entrance fee. *DeLorme: Ohio Atlas & Gazetteer:* Page 52, D-1

The legacy of deforestation and destruction so familiar to regions of southern Ohio found its way to the eastern portions of the state as well. The area that now encompasses Atwood Lake Park, near Carrollton, felt the brunt of the logging and mining practices that formed an integral part of the history of this state. Clear cutting left entire counties as lunar landscapes of rocks and bare soil. Environmentally, these areas were doomed. There was no wildlife to speak of and what was left of the productive soil was washed away with each rain. Without any vegetation to absorb the rainwater or hold the soil in place, the hills of eastern Ohio were subjected to severe erosion.

Even worse, river flooding had already been a problem long before the hills were cleared. Every spring the Muskingum River and its tributaries jumped their banks causing damage to enormous parts of the area. In this hilly region of the state few floodplains existed to take the brunt of the annual high waters. And those few areas with floodplains were usually developed for houses or agriculture. With no vegetation to hold things

together, rainwater simply flowed downhill. Whole towns were submerged by water and crops washed away before residents even knew what hit them.

In 1933 the Muskingum Watershed Conservancy District was formed to put an end to the deluging. The MWCD purchased over 54,000 acres of land in 18 different counties and went to work. When the MWCD designated 4,500 acres of land and water for Atwood Lake, it had no idea that the lake would become a weekend vacation spot for thousands of Ohioans every year. When it was built in 1937, the Atwood Dam was merely designed to control flooding around Indian Fork Creek. But the savvy MWCD soon realized that the dams, lakes, and other lands in the district could be used for more than just flood control, and expanded its role to include conservation and recreation. Today visitors to Atwood Lake can hike or ride the wooded trails, mingle with the reintroduced wildlife, camp at one of the 500 campsites, hang out at the beach, or cruise the waters in sailboats, paddleboats, rowboats, or powerboats.

Fire tower.

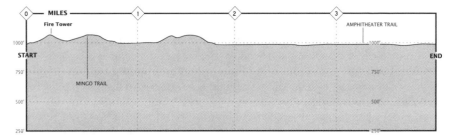

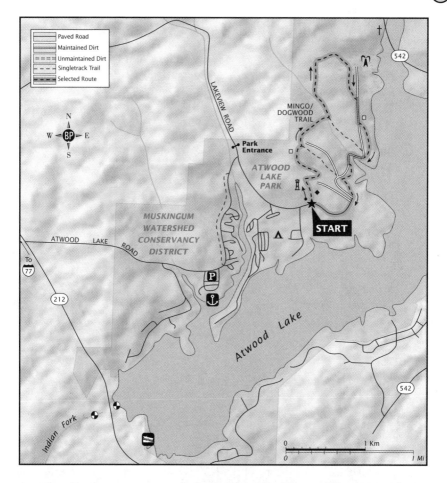

MilesDirections

0.0 START at the hiking trail to the left of the main drive about a half-mile into park. Climb immediately toward the fire tower.

0.2 Pass the fire observation tower.

0.5 Turn left on Mingo and Dogwood Trail.

0.8 This is a fast, yet gentle descent followed by a climb.

1.7 Cross the dirt service road.

2.0 Begin a fast, wide-open downhill. Watch out for the service road crossing about halfway down, as it's pretty treacherous with deep ruts perpendicular to the trail.

2.3 Ride through a swampy section at the bottom of the hill. It can be wet and muddy.

2.8 The trail comes to a clearing with an oil well, then follows a road for about 200 yards before jumping back into the woods to the left. When you hit the gravel road again, turn left.

3.0 Jump back on the Mingo Trail to your left.

3.3 Turn left onto the Amphitheater Trail.

3.4 Go straight across the field then climb back onto the singletrack.

3.9 Finish at the beginning of the hiking area.

Ride Information

● Trail Contacts:
Muskingum Watershed
Conservancy District
New Philadelphia, OH
(330) 343-6647

● Schedule:
Labor Day to Memorial Day

● Fees/Permits:
Park entrance is $5 per car and $1
per bike. Park at the Marina West to
save money.

● Local Information:
Muskingum Watershed
Conservancy District
New Philadelphia, OH
(330) 343-6647

● Local Events/Attractions:
Boat rentals at
Atwood Marina West
Mineral City, OH
1-800-882-6339

● Accommodations:
Atwood Lake Resort
and Conference Center
Dellroy, OH
1-800-362-6406

Atwood Lake Park (camping)
Mineral City, OH
(330) 343-6780

● Local Bike Shops:
Ernie's
New Philadelphia, OH
(330) 343-4056

● Maps:
USGS map: Mineral City, OH

Thanks to the efforts of the MWCD, erosion on the hill overlooking Atwood Lake is no longer a major concern. And the design of the trails along this hill ensures that drainage runs well. Except for the initial ascent past the fire tower, all of the trails climb and descend at a gentle grade so water will not flow straight down them. The only areas that get really muddy are short sections on the backside where a trail crosses a rutted access road and a swamp. In addition to minimizing erosion, the gentle grades make for fun riding.

Atwood Lake is visible from a couple of points along the trails. For the most part, though, the riding is through the thick woods where visibility is kept to a tunnel of trees. Although the trails are used for hiking, few people venture beyond the climb to the fire tower and ridge. Even on busy weekends riders will probably see few people on the Mingo and Dogwood Trails, both of which venture up and over the ridge. Keep in mind that the park charges $5 for every car to enter the park. If you're only there to ride, park at the marina and take the bike trail through the woods to the park entrance. It only costs a buck to enter by bike.

22

Bear Creek

Ride Summary

Bear Creek is home to a patchwork of trails stretching from the south side of Canton to the small town of Bolivar. There are three different sections of trail described below. The north section is the most extreme, with steep drops, tough climbs, and some fun jumps. The middle section offers gentler terrain, but the climbs can still be grueling. The south section is flatter and faster and follows ORV trails along Bear Run Creek.

Ride Specs

Start: Gravel road one mile south of Downing Street
Length: 13.3-mile loop
Approximate Riding Time: 2½ hours
Difficulty Rating: Technically difficult due to steep climbs, descents, and technical trails
Trail Surface: Doubletrack and singletrack
Lay of the Land: Hilly
Elevation Gain: 506 feet
Land Status: Public
Nearest Town: Canton
Other Trail Users: ORVs and hunters

Getting There

From Canton: Head south on I-77 to the exit for Fohl Street. Turn left on Fohl Street. Drive for about two miles then turn right on Dueber Avenue. About 5.5 miles from the intersection of Dueber Avenue and Fohl Street there is a gravel road on the left. Park in the grassy clearing at the intersection. *DeLorme: Ohio Atlas & Gazetteer.* Page 51, C-7

You'll never make it if you try to ride through.

ecause there are few trails in the Cleveland and Akron metro areas, riders often head south of Canton to the Bear Creek trails. These trails, originally developed by motorcycles, consist of a maze of doubletrack, oftentimes going straight up and down the hills. This isn't as much of a problem as in other ORV areas of Ohio as the hills here are not quite as big as those to the south. And many of the up-and-down trails here at Bear Creek have alternate routes that go around the really steep stuff should you choose to opt out of heavy climbing.

Like other motorcycle trails in the state, the Bear Creek trails can get very muddy. The clay soil is apt to stick to bike wheels and components, easily adding 20 pounds to your load. The mud will jam between your tires and brakes to quickly make the ride a stop-and-go affair requiring frequent dismounts to sling off the muck. It's sometimes so thick that rugged four-wheel-drive vehicles can be found mired in several feet of mud after a rain.

MilesDirections

0.0 START at the gravel road about one mile south of Downing Street (there are no street signs).

0.1 Enter the trail directly across from the gravel road.

0.3 At the small plateau on the hill, take a left onto the singletrack trail.

0.4 Cross a small clearing with a pump station in the middle. On the far side of the clearing, take the middle trail.

0.6 At the top of the hill, take the gravel road to the left.

0.7 Continue straight on the gravel road past another pump station.

0.8 Turn right on Gracemont Street.

0.9 Turn right onto the Pipeline Trail, which parallels the road.

1.1 Turn right at the gravel road by the gas well, then take an immediate left onto the singletrack.

1.5 At the driveway to the dump, go left across Gracemont Street and onto a dirt road.

1.8 Follow the trail at the end of the dirt road to the right.

2.9 After a clearing the trail turns left.

3.1 Cross underneath the dam road, then ride straight across the field.

3.3 On the far side of the field, the trail goes up the hill by the fence.

3.4 At the top of the hill, take the singletrack into the trees.

3.5 Turn right at North Orchard Road

3.8 Turn right on the spillway road and follow it all the way back to Gracemont Street.

4.1 Turn left onto Gracemont Street.

5.4 Turn right on Sherman Church Road.

7.4 Turn right on Haut Street.

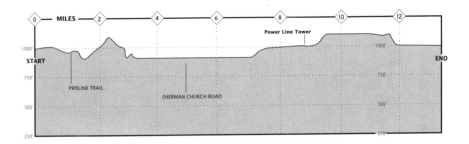

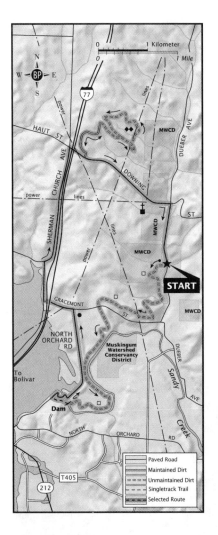

Ride Information

○ Trail Contacts:
Muskingum Watershed
Conservancy District
New Philadelphia, OH
(330) 343-6647

○ Schedule:
Closed November through April

○ Local Information:
Canton/Stark County
Convention and Visitors Bureau
Canton, OH
(330) 454-1439

○ Local Events/Attractions:
Stark County Bicycle Club
(weekly road and trail rides)
www.members.aol.com/starkscbc/
scbc/toc

○ Local Bike Shops:
Ernie's
Massillon, OH
(330) 832-5111

○ Maps:
USGS map: Bolivar, OH

7.6 At the top of the hill, turn left onto the gravel access road.

8.0 At the fork, follow the gravel road to the right.

8.1 Follow the dirt road at the left end of the clearing.

8.4 Turn left on the downhill trail.

8.5 Turn left onto a wide doubletrack trail.

8.7 Turn left at the power line tower.

9.2 At the top of the hill, turn left and follow the singletrack along the ridge.

9.3 At the three-way intersection, take the leftmost trail.

9.5 After crossing a small creek, turn left. There are lots of little hills to play on here before the trail begins to double back.

10.0 Turn right up the hill.

10.1 Turn right.

10.3 Turn left onto the gravel road.

10.9 Turn left on Haut Street, then right on Dueber Road.

13.3 End the ride at the gravel road.

Those who want to stay clean and preserve their expensive bikes may want to avoid this place after a rainfall.

The trails are divided into three sections. The northernmost section is just north of Haut Street. The trails here can be accessed east of Interstate 77 at the gravel road on top of the hill. This area is the most confusing of the three sections. Trails branch off in all directions from the gravel road. The trail along the power line is the easiest as it is mostly flat. From there it's a roller-coaster ride through woods and over steep drops with one sustained and somewhat technical climb to overcome. In the end, all the trails loop back to the beginning at the gravel road.

The middle section has a little more singletrack. This area can be accessed from Dueber Avenue (where the recommended ride begins). There is a very long and steep climb here, rewarded with a nice, long, off-camber descent. This is where you're likely to find trucks stuck in the mud. Hop on the singletrack and head south to Gracemont Street to access the Bolivar Dam trails.

The southernmost section, the Bolivar Dam area, is generally more gentle than the other sections, having only a few minor hills. There are, however, a couple of technical climbs that have been chewed up by dirt bikes. The trails follow a creek and may be underwater in the spring. This entire area is designated for flood control and the dam sometimes backs up when there are heavy rains. This is an out-and-back trail and does not form a loop.

Just down the road from the Bolivar Dam trails is the town of Bolivar and the gateway to Ohio Amish country. The Amish here are easily recognizable in their black horse-drawn buggies. Traditionally, the men wear white shirts and suspenders while the women have long dresses and bonnets. They don't use electricity or motorized vehicles, and candles light their way at night. They use horses to plow their fields and build their houses by hand. The Amish also operate quilt, furniture, and antique stores that make for interesting stops if you have time before or after your ride. The craftsmanship is often superb but most items are expensive. But the price is worth it—Amish beds, couches, and quilts are made to last for generations.

Madison Atchinson Property

Ride Summary

This trail, not far from Cleveland, may be short, but it's also a lot of fun. After a quick warm-up on the road, you'll turn onto the trail for a twisty ride along excellent single-track. There are plenty of areas to pick up momentum, and short ups and downs make it easy to maintain speed. For your technical fix (and a wicked descent), just head down the tricky descent to the river.

Ride Specs

Start: From the wooden gate on OH 307
Length: 2.9-mile loop
Approximate Riding Time: 30 minutes
Difficulty Rating: Difficult due to the tricky descent to the river, but moderate if this downhill is avoided
Trail Surface: Singletrack and double-track
Lay of the Land: Rolling, wooded hills with a steep drop to the Grand River
Elevation Gain: 313 feet
Land Status: County park
Nearest Town: Chardon
Other Trail Users: None

Getting There

From Cleveland: Take I-90 east about 17 miles past Painesville. Exit at OH 528 and turn right. After about two miles, turn left on Bates Road. Turn right on Bailey Road about a mile later. Since there's no parking at the Atchinson trailhead, riders must leave their vehicles at Riverview Park, which is just down the street from the Bates Road/Baily Road intersection. To ride to the trail from the parking area, turn right out of the park on Bailey, take a right on Bates, then turn right again on OH 307. A wooden gate and a Lake Metroparks sign mark the trailhead. *DeLorme: Ohio Atlas & Gazetteer.* Page 32, C-3

T he Western Reserve, set amidst the rolling hills of Cleveland's east side, is home to the Atchinson Property, site of one of the first trail-access triumphs for mountain bikers in northeast Ohio. Established by the Northern Ohio Mountain Bike Association (NOMBA), these trails are located on the eastern edge of Lake County.

NOMBA has been fighting for mountain bikers' rights in Cuyahoga, Summit, and Medina Counties without success for several years. While officials in the Cuyahoga Valley Recreation Area allow bikes on the heavily trafficked Towpath Trail, they will not consider opening any trails surrounding the Towpath. Nor will Cleveland Metroparks (the organization controlling the parks in all three counties) consider opening any of the thousands of acres of its parkland to off-road riders. As a result, off-road

Grand River.

cyclists have developed a somewhat antagonistic relationship with park officials in the Cleveland metro area. Many simply defy the park service, venturing onto off-limits singletrack anyway. And more often than not, when the park service catches those pedaling illegally on parkland, they issue hefty fines and confiscate bikes, further inciting mountain bikers—and the downward cycle continues.

MilesDirections

0.0 START at the wooden gate on the south side of OH 307. This is the beginning of the Atchinson Property.

0.1 Turn right onto the singletrack trail.

0.4 The trail arrives at an open area then forks. Take the left fork into the woods.

0.5 Turn right on the expert trail.

0.6 Go right onto the main trail after a small climb.

0.7 Go right where the trail forks.

1.2 Turn left before the cliff (a good place to admire the views of the river).

1.3 Turn right down a very technical trail to the river.

1.5 The trail hits the river.

1.7 After turning around and climbing back up the hill, turn right onto the main trail.

2.4 Turn right before the downed tree.

2.5 Turn right at the field and head toward the road.

2.9 End at the wooden gate at OH 307 where the ride began. Hit the trails for some more riding or pedal back to the Riverview Park parking area and your car.

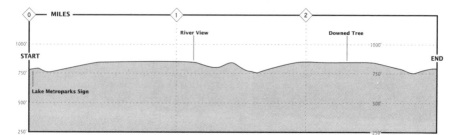

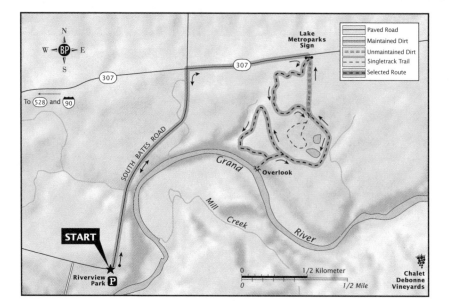

Ride Information

● Trail Contacts:

Lake County Metroparks
Mentor, OH
(440) 358-7275

NOMBA
Macedonia, OH
(330) 467-4751 or
www.ncweb.com/users/cbar

● Schedule:

Open year-round

● Local Information:

Lake County Visitors Bureau
Mentor, OH
1-800-368-5253 or
www.lakevisit.com

● Local Events/Attractions:

Grand River Wine Company
Madison, OH
(440) 298-9838

Chalet Debonne Vineyards
Madison, OH
(216) 466-3485

Ferrante Wine Farm
Geneva, OH
(216) 466-6046

● Maps:

USGS maps: Madison, OH;
Thompson, OH

Fortunately, in 1996, NOMBA gained some ground for off-road cyclists when the group decided to try its luck in sparsely populated Lake County to the east of the city. There, with the unexpected encouragement of county officials, they established the area's only legal singletrack on what is known as the Atchinson Property.

Though the trail system on the Atchinson Property is only about three miles in length, NOMBA did its best to utilize all of the area's natural features. As a result, the trail is fast, twisty, and very fun. At the beginning of the ride the trail drops down the slight slope toward the river, allowing for easy pedaling and fast but comfortable speeds. It twists in and out of the trees, making several loops suited for all types of riders. If you're looking for an easy ride, stay on top of the ridge overlooking the river. If you're looking for a little more adventure you may want to challenge yourself to the technical descent down to the river itself. Each loop is worth a run—if not for the trail riding excitement, then for the views of the Grand River valley.

When you're finished riding, take some time before heading home to explore the heart of Ohio wine country. The Grand River Wine Company and Chalet Debonne Vineyards are right around the corner from Atchinson. And not much further is the Ferrante Wine Farm. Ohioans are very proud of their wines, many of which have won awards in national and international contests. But don't expect the wines to taste the same as those from France, California, or Virginia. Ohio wines tend to be sweet, because the grapes they use flourish only in the soils of the Western Reserve.

Alpine Valley
Ski Resort

Ride Summary

Alpine Valley is home to some of the most technical mountain bike terrain in Northeast Ohio, offering approximately six miles of challenging grassy trails and ski slope hills. Rocks, roots, and mud challenge just about any rider, as do the steep climbs and descents of this summering ski resort. After you take a couple of easy laps to learn the course (which Alpine Valley officials change every week), you'll probably be able to ride the trail fast and enthusiastically for the rest of the day.

Ride Specs

Start: From the lodge at the base of the ski hill

Length: Approximately 3 miles

Approximate Riding Time: 30–45 minutes, depending on which course you follow

Difficulty Rating: Moderate to difficult due to steep climbs and fast descents

Trail Surface: Rocky singletrack and grassy ski slopes

Land Status: Private Ski Resort

Nearest Town: Chardon

Other Trail Users: Skiers

Getting There

From Cleveland: Take I-271 north to Mayfield Road (U.S. 322) and turn right. Alpine Valley is on the left, four miles after Mayfield Road crosses OH 306. Park at the lodge. *DeLorme: Ohio Atlas & Gazetteer.* Page 32, D-1

L
ike Mount Snow, Mammoth Mountain, Vail, and other ski areas across the nation, Alpine Valley has realized that life does not necessarily end when the snow stops falling. This local Cleveland ski area, which in winter receives more snow than almost any other resort in Ohio, has graciously opened its slopes in the summer to mountain biking, helping to supplement its income year-round. As a result, Alpine Valley is now home to some of the best riding in northeast Ohio.

The trails, which change every week, usually mix field and ski-slope riding with stretches of wooded singletrack. Epic ascents are not generally found in Ohio, but the folks at Alpine Valley have done a good job putting in some of the longest, most grueling climbs in the state. The climbs consist of both rocky, root-riddled, technical affairs and wide-open, steep ski slopes, all of which are guaranteed to cause any rider to suffer the joys of tough off-road bicycling.

Alpine Valley Ski Resort Mountain Snow Stats

Alpine Valley Ski Resort hosts downhill skiing and snowboarding during the winter months, its season typically lasting from mid-November through mid-March; www.alpinevalleyohio.com

Base Elevation: *1260 ft*
Summit Elevation: *1500 ft*
Vertical Drop: *230 ft*
Annual Snowfall: *120 in*
Night Skiing: *Yes*

Number of Lifts: *7*
Number of Trails: *10*
Longest Run: *2000 ft*
Skiable Area: *72 acres*
Snowmaking: *100%*

The rocks make this trail very fun.

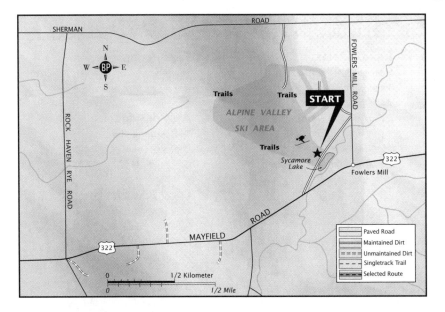

MilesDirections

No particular directions are given for this ride because the route changes from week to week. Alpine Valley officials and NOMBA volunteers change the course for every race.

But never fear. The suffering that takes place on the resort's climbs is always rewarded with awesome descents to ease the pain. The downhills, mostly along wooded singletrack, can typically be ridden at high speeds (if you're a fairly skilled cyclist). A couple of stretches, however, are particularly challenging, with rocky and off-camber sections that might send even the best riders into uncontrolled airtime. After these sections—reminiscent of some of the trails in West Virginia and Pennsylvania—come the ski-slope downhills. Most of these descents are interrupted by short sections of singletrack. The final downhill, though, is wide open and cyclists can bomb at 35 miles per hour plus.

The folks at Alpine Valley host nearly half-a-dozen races every summer on their slopes and surrounding woods. The racecourse is three miles in length and consists of a cross-country course with 50% single track and 50% ski slope hills and grassy trails. The competitions attract many of the best racers in the Cleveland area, and therefore draw other riders throughout northeastern Ohio to challenge themselves against the area's best.

179

Ride Information

🕐 Trail Contacts:

Alpine Valley Ski Resort
Chesterland, OH
(440) 285-2211 or
www.alpinevalleyohio.com

Northern Ohio
Mountain Bike Association
Macedonia, OH
(330) 467-4751

🕐 Schedule:

Open rides are May through October
on Wednesdays from 4:00 PM until
dusk and on Sundays from 12:00
PM until dusk. (No open ride on
Sunday, September 5th, 1999).

$ Fees/Permis:

There is a $4.00 trail fee. A helmet
and a signed waiver is required.

🏠 Accommodations:

Tri-Country Kamp Inn
Chardon, OH
(216) 968-3400

🚲 Local Bike Shops:

Bike Line
Broadview Heights, OH
(440) 546-9966
www.ohiobikeline.com

Ⓝ Maps:

USGS map: Chesterland, OH

Ohio Winters

It is winter. As the hours of daylight dwindle, the earth cools and cold winds begin to blow from far to the north, working their way south across the Canadian Plains. By the time they reach the United States they are full-fledged cold fronts carrying blustery winds, snow, and the dreary weather that typifies Midwestern winters. But for Chesterland, Ohio, home to Alpine Valley Ski Area, winter cold fronts are a great deal more than blustery weather. The ski area lies in the heart of the Ohio snow belt, seeing up to 176 inches of snow per year (compared with the 46-inch average of the rest of the state.) This snow belt is a result of something called the "lake effect." As winds from the northwest blow across Lake Erie they pick up considerable amounts of moisture, which is then dropped in the form of snow when it hits land. This translates into some of the best snow in Ohio—perfect for skiers anxious to break out their boards and do some snow riding.

Racers can also collect points toward the NOMBA/Alpine Valley series. All of these races help to benefit the Northeast Ohio Mountain Bike Association, which has done quite a bit to open trails to mountain bikers on both private and public lands in the region. NOMBA has also been a great support to the social scene as it helps bring local cyclists together with group rides.

Peace in motion.

Vulture's Knob

Ride Summary

This is one of the most technical and fun rides in the state. Riders need to be attentive at all times. Even the fast and seemingly easy sections have jumps and drops that can catch an unsuspecting rider off guard. The climbs are steep at times, as are the descents. Just for fun the trail builders have thrown in log crossings, log hops, and jumps. But the trail is fast overall and flows very well. Northern Ohioans have got to check this trail system out.

Ride Specs

Start: Picnic shelter off Mechanicsburg Road
Length: 6.9 miles
Approximate Riding Time: 1 hour
Difficulty Rating: Moderate to difficult due to steep climbs, log crossings, and switchbacks
Trail Surface: Singletrack and fire roads
Lay of the Land: Mostly singletrack with technical descents, climbs, and obstacles
Elevation Gain: 776 feet
Land Status: Private
Nearest Town: Wooster
Other Trail Users: Hunters

Getting There

From Medina: Take OH 3 south to Smithville Western Road. Turn right and cross over OH 83. At Mechanicsburg Road turn left and drive for about half a mile until you come to a fenced gravel road on the right. Often there is a bike-related poster on the fence. Turn right and drive to the picnic shelter.

From Wooster: Take OH 83 north to Highland Road. Turn left and go to Mechanicsburg Road. Take a right and continue for about a mile. The gravel road leading to the picnic shelter is on the left. *DeLorme: Ohio Atlas & Gazetteer.* Page 50, B-3

For years mountain bikers in the Cleveland metro area have been searching for legal trails to quench their off-road thirsts. Occasional oases have popped up only to follow a vicious cycle of overuse, degradation, public controversy, and ultimately, closure. This has left riders with two options: 1. Cruise the flat, boring expanses of towpath in the Cuyahoga Valley; or 2. Ride sweet, albeit illegal, trails in the metro parks while trying to avoid overworked rangers (and hefty fines), angry hikers, and equestrians.

But relief has arrived. About one hour south of downtown Cleveland an oasis, similar to the Atchinson Property in Madison County, has sprung that will surely belie the mirage status that has plagued other northeast Ohio trails. This choice riding spot is known as Vulture's Knob.

The Goldfish Hole.

The trail is about four miles north of Wooster, a town known mostly for its institute of higher learning, the College of Wooster. The college is the center of culture and learning in a town that has otherwise avoided the urban/suburban blight that is affecting areas to the north. Agriculture is the primary economic driving force, and its influence is evident in the local culture.

To get to the trail you have to drive for about one mile through a farmer's corn and soybean field, wondering if this is in fact the right place. But the field yields to a small stand of oak trees then the picnic shelter, marking the beginning of the trail.

MilesDirections

0.0 START from the picnic shelter and go north. (The trail can be ridden in both directions.)

0.4 The trail turns left and up a slight incline along an old dirt road.

0.5 Turn right, back onto the singletrack.

0.6 Turn left at the clear-cut at the bottom of the hill.

0.7 Stay to the left.

0.8 The trail turns right into a field with small trees.

1.0 Go left up the hill through the field.

1.2 Turn left into the woods.

1.3 Turn right then immediately left.

1.5 Turn right onto the gravel road.

1.6 Continue straight.

1.7 Turn left onto the road.

1.8 Go left, continuing on the ridge top.

2.0 The trail goes left along the top of a ravine.

2.1 Cross a rickety (but stable) bridge, then descend.

2.2 Climb left up Todd O's Detour.

2.3 Turn right, then climb the power line.

2.4 Turn right onto the gravel road.

2.5 Follow the singletrack trail to the left.

2.5 Turn right, and downhill, on the gravel road.

2.6 Follow the singletrack trail to the left.

2.6 Follow the trail to the right into the trees.

2.7 Cross the Goldfish Hole log crossing.

3.0 Turn right down the hill on the doubletrack trail.

3.1 Turn right at the bottom of the hill toward McAffey Road.

3.2 Take a left on McAffey Road.

3.5 Go straight across Flickinger Road.

3.6 Turn right after the fence, just past the barn.

3.7 Ride through the tree known as "the Willow." Beware of the drop and sharp right-hand turn on the other side. Walk if you are timid.

MilesDirections *continued*

3.8 The trail turns left at Killbuck Creek.

4.1 Trail turns left away from the creek and across the swamp.

4.6 Climb the hill; a ravine is off to the right.

4.7 Ride downhill, keeping the ravine off to your right.

4.8 Climb to the right.

5.0 Ride downhill back toward the swamp.

5.4 Turn left onto the dirt road near the barn.

5.5 Cross Flickinger and get back on McAffey.

5.8 Go right at the spray-painted gas wells.

5.9 Follow the trail to the right.

6.0 Turn right at the top of the hill.

6.0 Go left down the hill.

6.1 At the bottom of "Fern Gully," go right up the hill.

6.2 Turn left at the top of the hill.

6.3 Veer right into the "Snake" and prepare for its "Dueling Logs" section.

6.4 Turn left after the snake.

6.5 The trail turns right, drops down a very short hill and into a gravel pit, then continues straight across to the "Rock Tunnel."

6.6 Enter the "Rock Tunnel."

6.7 Climb left and out of the "Rock Tunnel."

6.9 Finish the ride at the picnic shelter.

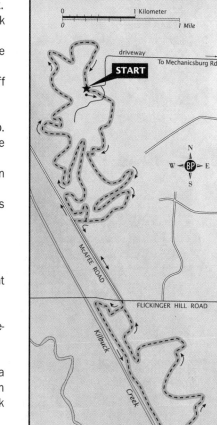

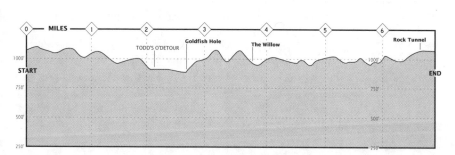

Ride Information

● Trail Contacts:
Mark or Paula Condry
Wooster, OH
(330) 264-7636
www.vulturesknob.com

● Schedule:
Open year-round; stay off the trails
when it's too sloppy.

● Fees/Permits:
Contributions of $3 are greatly
appreciated.

● Local Information:
**Wayne County Convention
and Visitor's Bureau**
Wooster, OH
1-800-362-6474
www.wooster-wayne.com

● Local Events/Attractions:
Vulture's Knob Race Schedules
www.vulturesknob.com/races.htm

● Restaurants:
The Barn
Smithville, OH

● Local Bike Shops:
Century Cycles
Medina, OH
(330) 722-7119

● Maps:
USGS map: Wooster, OH
Vulture's Knob Trail Map

Neither Todd Caldwell nor Mark Condry, the trail creators, had ever entered a mountain bike race when they cut the trails on their property in 1996. They just heard others talk about what a racecourse should have and cut the trail accordingly. Someone told them there should be at least one or two hike-a-bike sections, so they threw in a couple climbs that only the most skilled and determined riders can clean. Todd's background in BMX shows in the design of the course. It rewards riders who can muscle their bikes around tight turns, over logs, and through bar end–grabbing trees. The descents range from extremely technical, off-camber, switchback plunges that require every bit of a rider's skill and concentration to straight runs that are blazing fast. If you're inclined to leave the terra firma, there are even a few good jumps.

With a couple of years of trail maintenance and hosting races under their belts, Mark and Todd have perfected a formula for challenging yet enjoyable riding. The two can often be found out on the trail filling in mud holes, making jumps, clearing trees, and making treacherously narrow log bridges. In the fall they even blow leaves from the trail so that the course's perfect dirt surface remains exposed.

The amount of work, creativity, and consideration shows in the trails Mark and Todd cut. They seem to have a knack for making riders suffer and

each new section presents a new and often more difficult challenge for mountain bikers. Technical down-hills like the Rock Tunnel, Todd O. Detour, and Horseshoe Hill challenge the best bike handlers and are matched with even more difficult climbs. A few impossible switch-backs and log hops are thrown in for good measure.

Mark and Todd both have a great sense of humor, a fact that is particu-larly apparent at the Goldfish Pond, where a 12-inch-wide log bridge crosses a murky pond. It is void of any goldfish, or any other life forms for that matter, except for the occa-sional errant rider. Look out for Oh Shit, an innocent-looking drop-off that sends many riders over the bars; and the tabletop jump at the finish that often claims zealous pilots.

The main course is about four miles long, but the route is con-stantly changing and new trails have lengthened it to almost seven miles. The trail directions are meant solely as a guide and are by no means considered gospel. During the race season the trail is well marked so getting lost is not a problem. Just head south from the shelter and brace yourself for a roller-coaster ride on the best trail in northeast Ohio. You can ride the trails anytime, but Mark and Todd ask that you contribute $3 for every visit. They work on the honor sys-tem and $3 is not much considering the time and effort put into the trails and the enjoyment you'll get from riding them.

Considering races, Mark and Todd have foregone NORBA or other sanctioning bodies to offer a full schedule of events including night races, 24 Hour races and best of all, a Christmas tree race where all participants can chop their own tree.

When you're through, head to the Barn in Smithville for a wonderful $10 all-you-can-eat buffet. Just make sure you clean up some from your ride first. This is, afterall, a family place. It's a few miles east of Wooster on Smithville-Western Road.

Mohican Wilderness Campground

Ride Summary

This ride starts out with a steep climb on a gravel road, but quickly becomes fast and fun when it tops out on a ridge. There are several fast singletrack sections that thread tightly through the trees and some off-camber rock sections that will test any rider's skills.

Ride Specs

Start: Mountain bikers' parking lot on Walley Road
Length: 2.6-mile loop
Approximate Riding Time: 30 minutes
Difficulty Rating: Difficult due to steep climbs, sharp switchbacks, and technical descents
Trail Surface: Singletrack and gravel roads
Lay of the Land: Steep, wooded hills
Elevation Gain: 360 feet
Land Status: Private
Nearest Town: Loudonville
Other Trail Users: Hikers, equestrians, and hunters

Getting There

From Loudonville: Head south on OH 3 for about three miles. Turn left at Walley Road (there are signs for several campgrounds at the intersection). Continue on Walley Road for approximately eight miles. The mountain bikers' parking area is on the left, just after Mohican Wilderness Campground. *DeLorme: Ohio Atlas & Gazetteer.* Page 50, D-1

T hough this ride at the Mohican Wilderness Campground is less than three miles long, plenty of fun and challenging sections make it worthwhile. There are steep climbs, technical downhills, and plenty of fast sections to make any rider happy.

The worst part of this ride comes right at the start. After tracing around a small field, the trail goes straight up a very steep gravel road. This section can be ridden in your granny gear, but it is difficult. Deep gravel in some places makes it even worse. But this portion of the trail is short and soon enough the road turns into enjoyable, twisty singletrack.

Once on top of the ridge, the trail twists and turns through the trees and over roots and rocks. A couple of sections pass through a field and provide some of the ride's only open terrain. The field is essentially the top of the hill and the trail travels mostly downhill from there. High speeds can be

reached going downhill on the gravel road, but keep in mind that you'll be turning sharply to the right before the bottom of the road in order to catch the singletrack.

The singletrack constitutes the most technical section of the entire ride. There are several rocky sections that tend to bounce riders around and many trees that seem to reach for inattentive riders' handlebars. A couple of turns appear out of nowhere; if you miss them, you've got a date with the trees.

MilesDirections

0.0 START just across from the mountain bike parking lot and up the hill. Go left across the field and toward the woods. You may have to hop the fence.

0.1 When you get to the woods, turn right up the hill for a steep climb through the pine trees. At the top of the climb, turn right and follow the fence along the field.

0.2 Begin probably the most grueling climb of the course on this gravel road.

Grunt it out if you can because it's not that long. Walk if you must, just don't tell your friends. At the end of climb the trail switchbacks into the woods and is strewn with roots.

0.3 Begin a gradual climb.

0.5 After some generally rocky climbs and other assorted singletrack, climb along the power line to the field. At the beginning of the field take a left and follow the fence line.

MilesDirections *continued*

0.7 Turn left into the woods. Be prepared for lots of roots, rocks, and twisty single-track.

1.0 The trail turns right into a field then hops onto an old set of jeep tracks. You are now paralleling the road.

1.2 Turn right on the gravel road (if you go straight you'll end up in someone's driveway) and ride downhill.

1.4 Just before the intersection the trail takes a sharp right into the woods. It's very easy to miss.

1.6 Duck!

1.7 Test your rock-riding skills on this stone garden.

1.8 At the top of this climb you will again be at the field, but go left for a fun, fast, and rocky downhill with a couple of small creek crossings.

2.1 After cranking a long downhill, a sharp turn to the left takes you uphill.

2.2 Be prepared for a couple of switch-backs.

2.3 Caution: In the middle of this down-hill is a super-sneaky switchback that will definitely surprise you. A couple of trees await those who miss the turn.

2.4 After a creek crossing, there is a short climb with a somewhat tricky root at the top.

2.5 Turn left on the gravel road.

2.6 Finish at the field.

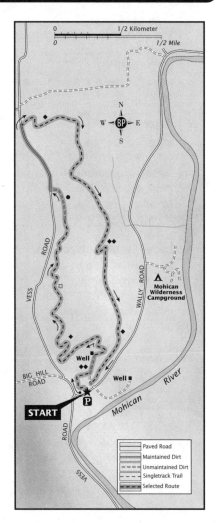

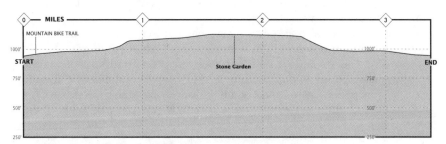

Ride Information

🕐 Trail Contacts:
Mohican Wilderness Campground
Glenmont, OH
(740) 599-6741
www.ohioparks.net/mohicanwilder-ness

🕐 Schedule:
March through November

❓ Local Information:
Mohican Tourist Association
Loudonville, OH
(419) 994-5225

💡 Local Events/Attractions:
Mid Ohio Mountain Bike Championship Series
Ryan O'Dell (419) 884-6100
www.mohican.net/vitals

Mohican Bluegrass Festival
Mohican Wilderness Campground
Glenmont, OH
(740) 599-6741
www.ohioparks.net/mohicanwilder-ness

Ohio Wine and Cheese Festival
October 2
Mohican Wilderness Campground
(740) 599-6741
www.ohioparks.net/mohicanwilder-ness

🚲 Local Bike Shops:
Ernies
Wooster, OH(330) 262-9003
www.erniesbikeshop.com

Ⓝ Maps:
USGS map: Greer, OH

Though named the Mohican Wilderness, this region was not named after the Mohican Indians. In fact, it was the Delaware Indians who called this area home and used it as a hunting ground. The region was originally referred to as Clear Fork, but was later named Mohican to distinguish it from the nearby Clear Fork State Park. Nevertheless, the Mohican Wilderness is a great place to spend a rustic weekend. The campsites are large and the facilities good. For those who don't like tent camping, log cabins are available. And there are plenty of activities for the family, including nature and crafts classes for the kids. The campground owns hundreds of acres of land perfect for hiking, biking, and horseback riding. In the fall it hosts the Mohican Bluegrass Festival, the Ohio Wine and Cheese Festival, Halloween parties, and hayrides.

The region's biggest draw is the Mohican River, which formed as a result of glaciation some 12,000 years ago. Thousands of people visit the area every year to canoe or tube down the river's lazy waters. It's a perfect way to relax, get some sun, or enjoy a cold beer. The Mohican Wilderness Campground rents canoes and hosts canoe races during the summer, but canoes can also be rented at most of the other campgrounds nearby.

Findley State Park

Ride Summary

This ride, boasting great scenery with wildflowers and a wildlife refuge, is a wonderful place to take a beginner on his or her first ride in the dirt. The trails, like the atmosphere of the park, are very mellow. Bring the family along and do some fishing when you're through cycling.

Ride Specs

Start: Boat launch parking lot on Park Road 4
Length: 3.3 miles
Approximate Riding Time: 30 minutes
Difficulty Rating: Easy due to the flat, wide trails
Trail Surface: Mostly doubletrack, with some singletrack and paved riding
Terrain: Mostly flat
Elevation Gain: 53 feet
Land Status: State park
Nearest Town: Wellington
Other Trail Users: Hikers

Getting There

From Wellington: Go south on OH 58 for approximately two miles. Turn left at the park entrance. Take the turning lane right to Park Road 3, then take the first left on Park Road 1. Turn right on Park Road 4 toward the boat launch and parking the lot. *DeLorme: Ohio Atlas & Gazetteer:* Page 40, D-1

This trail is great for initiating the beginner.

This three-mile, forested cruise around part of Findley Lake is great for novice cyclists looking to get their wheels dirty for the first time. The terrain, unlike most places elsewhere in the state, is decidedly mellow—perfect if you prefer to avoid gnarly hills, logs, rocks, or roots. Not surprisingly, this area of the state is not known for its mountain biking. It just doesn't present the variety and challenge that most cyclists prefer. It is, however, a popular place among riders with families. Kids and other non-mountain bikers often spend afternoons on the lakeshore fishing for bass, bluegill, and crappie while the riders in their families enjoy the trail.

Because the terrain is so harmless, this is the perfect place to initiate a new mountain biker to dirt. When the ride is over, cruise down to the beach for a picnic or rent a canoe, rowboat, or paddleboat and spend some time out on the water. At the end of the day pitch a tent at one of the many campsites and enjoy an evening under the stars.

MilesDirections

0.0 START from the restrooms at the end of the boat launch parking area.

0.1 Follow the Larch Trail to the left.

0.2 The Larch Trail crosses over Park Road 1 then, soon after, crosses the parking lot. Follow the trail marker on the opposite side of the parking lot.

0.4 Pass the beach.

0.5 Pass a concession stand then follow a gravel path past the rowboat launch.

0.6 The trail turns right into the woods.

0.7 Follow the trail marker to the right and cross the dam.

1.1 Descend into the spillway. The trail changes names to the Spillway Trail.

1.6 The trail splits. Follow the left fork to the road.

1.7 The Spillway Trail ends at Park Road 3 and the campground. Turn around and follow the trail back (or continue around the road to the boat launch area).

2.2 Cross the spillway.

2.7 Turn left onto Larch Trail, then veer right where the trail forks.

2.8 Pass the concession stand again.

2.9 The trail reenters the woods.

3.0 Take the Black Locust Trail to the right.

3.2 Turn right at the road and take the trail straight across from the stop sign.

3.3 Finish at the parking lot.

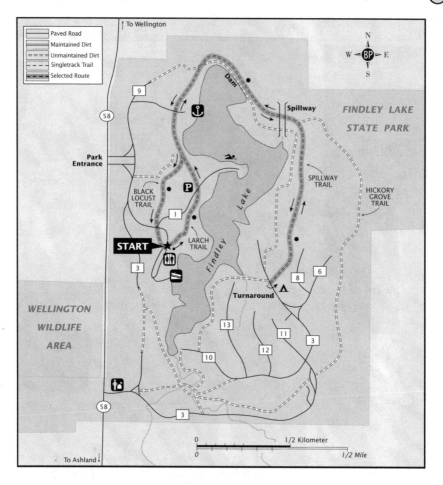

Those looking for wildlife can go to the Wellington Wildlife Area across the road (OH 58) to see deer, red fox, beavers, and raccoons. Wildflowers, including spring beauties, Dutchman's breeches, hepatica, bloodroot, marsh marigold, trillium, and woodland asters, bloom at various times of the year. In one area of the park visitors can see the extremely rare duke's skipper butterfly.

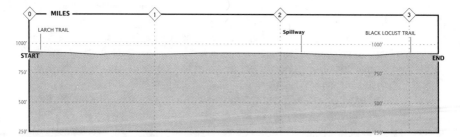

197

Ride Information

Trail Contacts:
Findley State Park
Wellington, OH
(440) 647-4490
www.ohioparks.net/findley

Schedule:
Open year-round

Local Information:
Lorain County Visitors Bureau
Lorain, OH
1-800-334-1673

Local Events/Attractions:
Archibald M. Willard exhibit
(Willard painted Spirit of '76)
Wellington Library
Wellington, OH
1-800-334-1673

Findley State Park (boat rentals)
Wellington, OH
(440) 647-4490

Accommodations:
Findley State Park (camping)
Wellington, OH
(440) 647-4490
www.ohioparks.net/findley

Local Bike Shops:
Century Cycles
Medina, OH
(330) 722-7119

Maps:
USGS maps: Wellington, OH;
Sullivan, OH

When you're not riding, fishing, boating, or picnicking, head over to nearby Wellington. The town is a throwback to the days of yore with quaint houses and streets lined with huge oaks. Nearly 75 percent of the downtown district, with its distinct New England architecture, is on the National Register of Historic Places. In 1807 the Connecticut Land Company sold 4,000 acres to four men from Massachusetts. This area is now Wellington Township. In 1818 William T. Wellington of Montgomery County, New York, came to the area and founded the town of Wellington with the original settlers from Massachusetts.

During the 1800s the town flourished with wagon and carriage shops and industries such as brick making. The wagon and carriage industries slowly declined with the coming of the railroad, but by that time cheese had established itself as the major moneymaker in the area. Dairy fields were everywhere, and at one time the area was considered to be one of the greatest cheese-producing locations in the Union. The county alone produced the equivalent of one pound of cheese per year for every person in the state. Today the area is still known as Ohio's dairy land.

In the midst of the Great Depression, Lorain County Common Pleas Judge Guy B. Findley purchased a tract of agricultural land two miles south

of the town of Wellington. He donated this land to the state of Ohio to be maintained as a state forest used for timber production and forestry experiments. With help from the Civilian Conservation Corps the land was sowed with nearly half a million trees. The land was later designated a state park in 1950 and today trails traverse much of that original forest sown more than 50 years ago.

Honorable Mentions

Northeast Ohio

Noted below is one of great rides in the Northeast region that didn't make the A-list this time around but deserves recognition nonetheless. Check it out and let us know what you think. You may decide that it deserves higher status in future editions or, perhaps, you may have a ride of your own that merits some attention.

Ⓛ Cuyahoga Valley Towpath

The Towpath, as it is known in Cleveland, is the weekend getaway for many active people. Bikes are allowed only on the limestone trail. Rangers will hand out hefty fines if you venture onto the singletrack that loops off the Towpath. The trail is about 20 miles from end to end and will be even longer sometime in the future—it may stretch from Cleveland to Canton some day.

The best access to the trail is in the village of Peninsula. Stop at Century Cycles on Main Street—by the railroad tracks—and they will tell you the best places to go. For information call the Cuyahoga Valley National Recreation Area at (216) 524-1497, or Century Cycles at (330) 657-2209. *DeLorme: Ohio Atlas & Gazetteer:* Page 41, C-6

Northwest

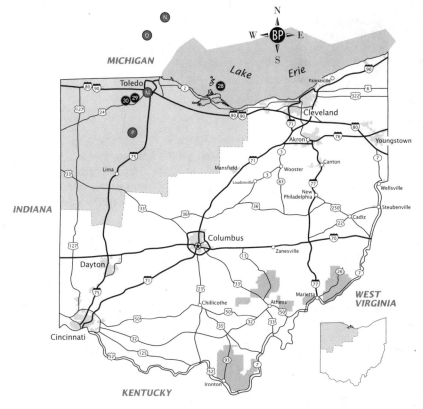

D uring the last ice age, which began about 1.65 million years ago, this region of Ohio was scoured by gigantic ice cubes that decapitated any hills and filled any valleys that may have once existed. As the glaciers receded and melted, much of Northwestern Ohio became a swamp. The Great Black Swamp was one of the last regions to be settled in the state. It was given its name because people believed that the swamp floor never saw the light of day. Many believed that any who entered the swamp would never return.

Mountain bikers have little to fear now. The swamp has long since been drained, and the only obstacle that presents itself to some smooth mountain biking is the corn stalk. The trail systems are relatively short, fast, and lack obstacles—hills or people. The trails of Kelley's Island, Maumee State Forest, and Mary Jane Thurston Park present you with some great views to compensate for the lack of terrain. Indeed, the rides featured in this section have less than 50 feet of elevation change.

Riders that crave singletrack with more elevation gain can make a short drive north across the border into Michigan. The trails highlighted in the honorable mentions section have been rated some of the best in the nation by the national cycling media.

Kelleys Island

Ride Summary

Kelleys Island is not really a mountain bike destination. The trails here are limited in both length and technical obstacles. But bikes are the best way to get around the island, so why not explore the trails while you're at it? There are two sections of trails on the island. The one on the north side is the most challenging and has the most singletrack. The middle section, by the quarry, is less challenging. But it's a great shortcut to the winery.

Ride Specs

Start: Neuman Boat Line dock in Marblehead
Length: Varies
Approximate Riding Time: Varies
Difficulty Rating: Easy due to the lack of hills
Trail Surface: Mostly doubletrack with few variations in elevation
Lay of the Land: Flat woodlands and fields
Nearest Town: Marblehead
Other Trail Users: Hikers

Getting There

From Port Clinton: Take OH 163 east to Marblehead. From Marblehead follow OH 163 and turn left at the custard stand onto Foot of Forces Street (you will see the billboard for the Kelleys Island Ferry). *DeLorme: Ohio Atlas & Gazetteer:* Page 28 D-4

M ost of the millions of people who visit the Lake Erie islands every year do not go to enjoy mountain bike adventures of the singletrack variety. They visit, quite frankly, to party at the largest bar in the world (on Put-In-Bay) or to escape for the weekend and sample wine at the vineyard on Kelleys Island (which can lead to biking adventures of another kind). Both the type of riding and the type of recreation most popular on the island are a direct result of the geography of the islands.

Thousands of years ago, as massive glaciers were forming the hills of southern and eastern Ohio, the northern area of the state was being wiped clean of any major geographic formations. The glaciers reduced the area to exposed bedrock in many places and their massive weight left deep depressions that eventually filled with meltwater—meltwater that now forms Lake Erie.

Cross bikes, mountain bikes— it's all good

Kelleys Island, three miles from mainland Ohio, was spared the wrath of the glaciers' weight. They did visit the island, however, and their presence is still visible. On the northern side of the island are rare formations known as glacial striations. These grooves form an eerie, almost purposeful linear pattern across the ground, as if they were carved by the hands of men, not the weight of glaciers. Years ago visitors could explore these grooves up close, but many chose to leave their initials on the rock. So today the area is fenced off and must be observed from a distance.

Long after the glaciers retreated, Ottawa, Huron, and Erie Indians occupied the islands. The most notable mark of their existence is left on Inscription Rock on the south side of the island. Petroglyphs more than 500 years old are carved in this massive limestone rock.

Many years later, after European occupation, the islands were the scene of historic naval battles during the war of 1812. The most notable battle was won by American Oliver Hazard Perry. With a fleet that was clearly outmatched by the British, Perry led his sailors to a decisive victory and coined the saying: "We have met the enemy and they are ours." The victory gave America control of the Great Lakes.

In 1854, J.D. Rivers purchased five of the islands and introduced 2,000 cattle to them. When that proved unsuccessful, he converted his land into fruit farms. The islands have the longest frost-free period in the state due to the stabilizing effect of the lake (essentially, the lake cools at a slower temperature, keeping the islands warmer longer than the mainland). Eventually, growing grapes became a very profitable enterprise for those living on the islands. By 1887, more than one-third of the grapes and nearly half of the wine in the entire state of Ohio were produced on the islands.

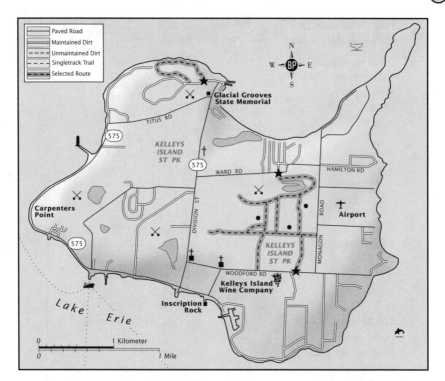

MilesDirections

Because this ride can be completed in many different ways and since local attractions might get you away from the bike, a detailed list of directions is not necessary—though you might need them after a few glasses of wine. Don't drink and ride.

Ride Information

 Trail Contacts:
Kelleys Island State Park
Kelleys Island, OH
(419) 746-2546 or
www.kelleysisland.com

 Schedule:
The ferry to Kelleys Island runs regularly from April to October from 8 a.m. to 11p.m.
Call (419) 798-5800

$ Fees/Permits:
The ferry costs $9 per adult ($5 for children) and an additional $3.50 per bike

? Local Information:
Kelleys Island
Chamber of Commerce
Kelleys Island, OH
(419) 746-2360

Local Events/Attractions:
Kelleys Island Wine Company
Kelleys Island, OH
(419) 746-2537

Glacial Grooves
Kelleys Island State Park
Kelleys Island, OH
(419) 746-2546

Restaurants:
Bag the Moon Saloon
Kelleys Island, OH
(419) 746-2365

The Casino
Kelleys Island, OH
(419) 746-2773

Local Bike Shops:
Sun & Surf
Kelleys Island, OH
(419) 746-2786 – *rentals available*

Kelleys Cove
Kelleys Island, OH
(419) 746-2622 – *rentals available*

Maps:
USGS maps: Kelleys Island, OH

Today, wineries are among the islands' main attractions. Tourists visiting the Kelleys Island Winery can enjoy several varieties of wine while sitting in the sun or relaxing on the patio with a platter of bread and cheese. It's an excellent place to refuel after half a day of exploring the island by bike.

Bikes are indeed the best way to explore the island, but by no means should Kelleys Island be considered a destination for mountain biking adventure. The terrain of the island is very flat and the trails are wide and decidedly non-technical. But they can be an excellent place for those just beginning to do some off-road cycling or for those hoping to bring the whole family along.

The East Quarry Trail is a good shortcut from the north side of the island to the Kelleys Island Winery. If fishing is your fancy, Horseshoe Lake is full of smallmouth bass and several species of sunfish.

The North Shore Loop Trail passes the North Quarry, where stone for buildings and bridges in Cleveland were produced.

Also along the trail is an old loader which was used to load rail cars with rock. The rocky shores of the lake are also accessible along several points along the trail.

The only way to get to Kelleys Island is by ferry. The most direct ferry runs from the town of Marblehead. The huge billboards on Ohio 163 will point you in the right direction. Cost of the ferry ride is $9 and an additional $3.50 for bikes. Bikes are by far the best and most economical way to get around the island. Cars are allowed but cost more to ferry and aren't very practical on the small island. Limited camping is available on the north side of the island in Kelleys Island State Park. You shouldn't need to stay overnight as a day should allow you to see most of the sights on the island. But an overnight stay under the stars on Kelleys Island is always a treat.

Maumee State Forest

Ride Summary

Don't expect a lot of climbing on this trail system. There is only a 15-foot elevation change in the entire Maumee State Forest. Riders can expect fast, sandy trails that are fairly wide because of the ORV traffic. ORV riders have also cut a maze of trails through the forest. Getting lost is not a problem because all the trails form loops, but don't count on following the same trail twice. Notice the perfect rows of pines as you pedal along. This area was planted as a windbreak more than 50 years ago.

Ride Specs

Start: ORV trailhead on Indian Reservation Road (CR 1)
Length: About 5 miles, depending on which trails you ride
Approximate Riding Time: 1 hour
Difficulty Rating: Easy to moderate due to fast, sandy sections and a lack of elevation change
Trail Surface: Doubletrack and singletrack
La of the Land: Flat and sandy
Elevation Gain: 15 feet
Nearest Town: Whitehouse
Other Trail Users: Off-road vehicles and hunters

Getting There

From Waterville: Head west on OH 64. When the road turns right, continue straight on Waterville/Swanton Road. At the county line Waterville/Swanton becomes Archbold Lutz Road. Don't be confused. Just continue straight until you get to Indian Reservation Road (CR 1), then turn left. The ORV parking lot is on the left. ***DeLorme: Ohio Atlas & Gazetteer:*** Page 26, D-1

The Toledo area is cursed by the fact that there are no hills in the area to speak of. The landscape was wiped flat by glaciers thousands of years ago. Where significant elevation changes do occur, the troughs are typically filled with water such as Lake Erie and the Maumee River. Factor in suburban sprawl and agriculture occupying much of the non-flooded land, and there leaves little dry land open to the public. Even worse, most places that do have parks in this area have declared mountain biking off-limits. This leaves little terrain for local off-road riders.

Fortunately, cyclists can get a break at Maumee State Forest. It's one of only two legal trail systems in the Toledo area.

When this area was settled in the mid-1800s developers drained a major swamp and cleared the surrounding forests. When they were through, all

that was left was miles and miles of bare ground. The sandy soil that remained was highly susceptible to wind-caused erosion.

To combat the erosion, the Forest Service stepped in to plant windbreaks. Projects like this were popular during the Depression era. The federal government spent millions of dollars to employ down-on-their-luck men through the Civilian Conservation Corps. It was CCC workers who helped plant the trees that grow in Maumee State Forest today.

East of County Road 1 a short loop trail cuts its way through an oak forest. The most prominent trees in Maumee, however, are pines, and neat rows of the evergreens cover most of the terrain west of the county road. This is also where most of the park's best (and least eroded) singletrack trails are found.

Ride Information

◕ Trail Contacts:
Maumee State Forest
Swanton, OH
(419) 822-3052
www.itown.net/Forests/maumee

◔ Schedule:
Open year-round, except during hunt-
ing season. Contact Maumee State
Forest for specific dates.

❓ Local Information:
**Greater Toledo Convention
and Visitor's Bureau**
Toledo, OH
1-800-243-4667

◉ Local Events/Attractions:
Sauder Museum Farm and Village
Archbold, OH
(419) 446-2541

Toledo Mudhens Baseball
Toledo, OH
(419) 893-9483

Toledo Museum of Art
Toledo, OH
(419) 255-8000

◉ Local Bike Shops:
Bikeworks
Sylvania, OH
(419) 882-0800

Ⓝ Maps:
USGS map: Swanton, OH

Forest Rules

- *Maumee State Forest is open to visitors between the hours of 6 a.m. and 11 p.m. daily.*

- *Hunting is permitted within Maumee State Forest in accordance with Division of Wildlife regulations.*

- *Snowmobiles, motorcycles, and mountain bikes are permitted in the All-Purpose Vehicle Area.*

- *Horseback riding is permitted only along roads or on designated bridle trails.*

- *Camping and building of fires is prohibited.*

- *Disturbance, defacement or destruction of any property, material, natural feature or vegetation is prohibited. Berries, nuts and mushrooms may be gathered and removed from state forest land.*

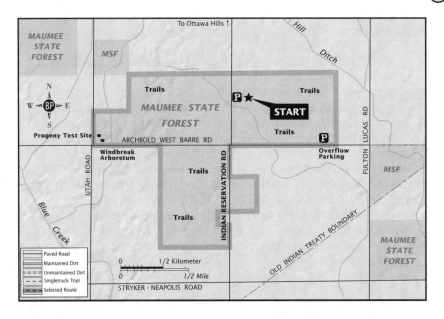

MilesDirections

Much like Alum Creek, the trails at Maumee State Forest crisscross through the ORV area, making the task of giving specific directions daunting. Therefore, just ride wherever your wheels take you.

Cutting through the forest, the main loop's trails are very wide. In fact, motor vehicles have traveled them enough to turn them into full-fledged roadways. With few obstacles in the way, these roads can be ridden at very high speeds. And, with lots of small whoop-de-doos, they also happen to be great for catching air.

If you're looking for singletrack, your best bet is to follow any of the many offshoots from the main loop trails. Again, motorcycles have made these trails wide enough to cruise without fear of getting tangled in undergrowth or snagged by errant tree limbs.

Given the terrain (or lack thereof), these trails are not that bad. The elevation changes less than 15 feet across the entire forest, but there are enough trails for everyone—beginners and experts alike—to get a decent workout.

The Toledo Strip

In 1835 the City of Toledo almost had the dubious distinction of being the site of the first civil war in the United States.

The original border between Michigan and Ohio was known as the Ordinance Line–designated by the Northwest Ordinance of 1787–and was later altered by the Fulton Line (1818) and the Talcott Line (1834). The Fulton and Talcott Lines practically coincided with each other and ran a straight course due east from the southernmost tip of Lake Michigan (south of Maumee Bay), striking the south-western shore of Lake Erie after having passed a few miles south of Toledo. The U.S. Attorney General even told President Andrew Jackson that this was the correct border between the State of Ohio and the territory of Michigan.

Ohio, when petitioning Congress for statehood in 1802, surveyed a new line that was north of the previously accepted Talcott Line, and somewhat similar to the present day Michigan-Ohio state line. The section of land between the new border and the Talcott Line totaled about 450 square miles and became known as the Toledo Strip. It was a wedge-shaped strip five miles wide at the Indiana border and eight miles wide at Lake Erie.

Michigan was terribly upset with the turn of events. Not only had it lost 450 square miles of territory, it had also lost what is now known as Maumee Bay, one of the best harbors on the Great Lakes. To show their disdain for the treatment, parties of Michigan Militia performed frequent raids on Toledo and the surrounding areas.

The situation became so heated that Ohio Governor Lucas marched his troops toward Toledo in June of 1835. At the same time, Michigan troops were marching south to meet the Ohio forces. A battle seemed imminent.

On the night of June 8, 1835, Governor Lucas made a bold move that would push the two states even closer to war. He created Lucas County out of part of Wood County and sent judges in the middle of the night to appoint commissioners and other personnel. With that, Lucas could prove jurisdiction and legally claim Toledo for the state of Ohio.

The leaders of Michigan were furious. It took interference by the United States Congress and President Jackson to avert serious conflict. On June 15, 1836 Congress passed an act admitting Michigan into the Union once it surrendered the Toledo Strip to Ohio. The U. S. Congress was, in effect, holding Michigan's petition for statehood hostage.

As a compromise for the messy affair, Congress would add the western three-quarters of the Upper Peninsula to Michigan's borders. Although unknown at the time, the 9,000 square miles given to Michigan would become some of the nation's most valuable copper, timber, and iron producing land.

Although it might seem odd that President Jackson and Congress gave the Toledo Strip to Ohio when it clearly belonged to Michigan, it was in Jackson's best political interests to do so. The 1836 Presidential election was close at hand, and the National Democratic Party looked forward to Ohio's electoral votes. Michigan, as a territory, had no electoral votes to give.

Michigan citizens were extremely upset with the turn of events and initially voted not to become a state in the Union. But statehood was very important to Michigan, as were the benefits inherent in statehood. As a state, Michigan would be in a position to share in the surplus for internal improvements. After a second vote on December 14, 1836 Michigan voted to become a state. It was formally admitted into the Union as the nation's twenty-sixth state on January 26, 1837.

15 feet of vertical, courtesy of the last ice age

Mary Jane Thurston State Park

Ride Summary

The trails at Mary Jane Thurston State Park are relatively easy due to the flat terrain bordering the Maumee River. Almost all of the trails follow North Turkeyfoot Creek or the Maumee, so be sure to take the time to stop, relax, and listen to the soothing sound of flowing water. During fishing season bring a rod and cast for walleye. All of the trails are loops, so getting lost is not a problem.

Ride Specs

Start: Pheasant Loop trailhead on the east side of OH 24, just north of North Turkeyfoot Creek
Length: 6 miles
Approximate Riding Time: 30–60 minutes
Difficulty Rating: Easy due to the flat terrain
Trail Surface: Singletrack
Terrain: Wooded riverside singletrack and doubletrack
Elevation Gain: 74 feet
Land Status: State park
Nearest Town: Napoleon
Other Trail Users: Hikers and hunters

Getting There

From Maumee: Follow OH 24 south. The North Turkeyfoot area of Mary Jane Thurston State Park is about 15 miles south of Waterville, just past the village of Texas. Park at the Pheasant Loop trailhead on the left side of the highway. *DeLorme: Ohio Atlas & Gazetteer.* Page 36, A-1

Mary Jane Thurston State Park lies in what was the final frontier of Ohio—the Black Swamp. The Black Swamp is a 120-by-40-mile strip of land roughly following the Maumee River from Toledo, south toward Van Wert, and more or less up the Ohio-Indiana state line. The low-lying Maumee River valley was left as a giant mud hole after the glaciers receded, and was at one time so murky and mosquito infested that people doubted it would ever be inhabitable.

Though the swamp has since been cleared to accommodate agriculture and settlement, its legacy is still visible at Mary Jane Thurston State Park. The flat floodplain occupied by the North Turkeyfoot area can be very swamp-like when the spring rains come. In the spring of 1997 the Maumee overflowed its banks and left much of the park underwater. Homes along the banks of the river became islands unto themselves.

While the flood of 1997 was not typical, it's still a good idea to call ahead before setting out on a ride through the park. You never know when the

I know the trail is here somewhere.

MilesDirections

0.0 START at the Pheasant Loop Trailhead.

0.1 Turn left at the old granary onto the Pheasant Loop Trail.

0.2 Turn right at the first parking lot heading south.

0.3 At the creek, follow the Pheasant Loop Trail to the right.

0.7 Continue past the granary and turn left on the Red Fox Trail.

0.8 Cross the bridge, then turn right on Whitetail Loop.

1.5 Turn left at the intersection, heading south.

1.7 Turn left at the Maumee River.

2.6 Turn left on the Red Fox Trail.

2.8 Veer left onto the Raccoon Loop.

3.2 Return to the Red Fox Trail and go right.

3.4 Turn left on the Whitetail Loop at the river.

4.1 The trail goes left at North Turkeyfoot Creek.

4.9 Turn right on the Red Fox Trail.

6.0 Finish at the parking lot.

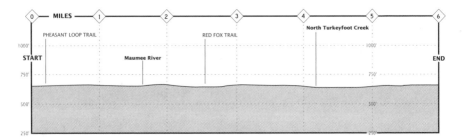

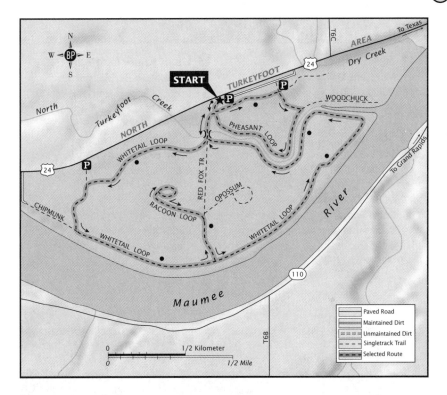

next major deluge will arrive. If it turns out the trails are wet when you visit, turn in your bike for a fishing rod and try your hand at catching walleye. The park, including the North Turkeyfoot area, is an excellent place to cast a line. The Maumee River is known nationwide as one of the best places in North America to fish for walleye. The white-bass fishing is also good.

When the trails are dry they can be fast and fun. There is little elevation change here and technical challenges are few and far between, so beginners will find plenty to keep them happy on the six miles of the area's trails. But skilled and fit riders can also have fun, as it's easy to pick up speed and a couple of laps can provide a good workout. While most of the riding is confined to the woods, some of the trails follow the river and include excellent views.

The North Turkeyfoot area gets its name from a Native American chief who participated in the Battle of Fallen Timbers not far from where the park lies today. The battle was one of the most significant in the United States' history. For the U.S., control of this area was vital to the country's survival. The addition of the Northwest Territory would permit the United States to grow beyond its original 13 states, and monies gained from the sale of this land would pay the Revolutionary War debts that threatened to bankrupt the government.

Ride Information

 Trail Contacts:
Mary Jane Thurston State Park
McClure, OH
(419) 832-7662

Schedule:
Open year-round, except during hunting season

Local Information:
Grand Rapids
Chamber of Commerce
Grand Rapids, MI
(419) 832-1106

 Local Events/Attractions:
Canoeing on the Maumee River
from the Bend to Perrysburg
Contact the Division of Watercraft
(614) 265-6506

Shawnee Princess (boat ride)
Grand Rapids, MI
(419) 531-0341

Maps:
USGS Maps: Colton, OH; Napolean East, OH

The Black Swamp

With victory at the Battle of Fallen Timbers, the Black Swamp region and nearby Toledo were finally open for settlement. Although Ohio had become a state in 1803 and other parts of the Midwest had already opened up, travelers approaching the swamp made tracks south to avoid the mosquito-infested forest. Rumors spread about travelers who entered the swamp to travel through and were never seen again.

The first successful Black Swamp settlers made their way to Lauber Hill, in Fulton County, in 1834. They almost starved to death during their first winter, in part because they had not brought guns with them. However, nearly 10 years later these same settlers managed to dig 100 miles of drainage ditches by hand with shovels full of the heavy mud. This helped to open up the area and logs were laid side by side to create a roadway over which to travel. But this would not last long as the mucky earth soon swallowed the road up.

Today, little of the swamp remains. In its place are small towns and thousands of acres of farmer's fields. The only legacy of the Black Swamp may be with the floods that come each spring as the muddy Maumee overflows its banks and swallows up the land once again, if only for a few days.

Great Britain also had an interest in the land as it generated great fur-trading revenues. They supported the Native Americans, if not for furs, then for fear the Native Americans might turn on the Canadian frontier. The Indians, however, were fighting for the last of their land and for their own survival.

After two humiliating defeats to Native American warriors, the pride of the U.S. Army was at stake. Hundreds of troops had been lost and the army was ridiculed both at home and abroad. But General "Mad" Anthony Wayne was not about to lose. He had prepared his troops for months leading up to the fateful Battle of Fallen Timbers.

On the morning of August 20, 1794, Wayne's army encountered a force of about 1,100 Native Americans backed by a handful of British volunteers. At first the American front line was driven back, but soon they were reinforced by more soldiers waiting in a jumble of trees uprooted by a recent tornado.

Among the legendary heroes surfacing from the battle was Chief Turkeyfoot, the only individual from either side in the conflict to be honored with a monument. Turkeyfoot Rock stands in his memory. The North Turkeyfoot area of Mary Jane Thurston State Park is also named for him. Oddly, however, there is no historical proof that Turkeyfoot ever actually existed.

Honorable Mentions

Northwest Ohio

Compiled here is an index of great rides in Northwest Ohio that didn't make the A-list this time around but deserve recognition. Check them out and let us know what you think. You may decide that one or more of these rides deserves higher status in future editions or, perhaps, you may have a ride of your own that merits some attention.

(M) Sidecut Metropark

This easy trail follows an old canal. This is a great place to take beginners and introduce them to the sport. Everyone will enjoy the scenery. There are a couple of singletrack trails that detour off the limestone trail, but they are not very long.

From Maumee, take River Road to the first parking area on the left at Sidecut Metropark. The trail begins near the road on the left side as you are entering the parking lot. For information call (419) 535-3050. *DeLorme: Ohio Atlas & Gazetteer*: Page 26, D-3

(N) Pontiac Lake, Michigan

This 10-mile trail is a roller coaster ride. There are few sustained climbs and the downhills are fast. Rocks, roots, and drop-offs make things technical but don't slow you down too much. This is a seriously fun ride.

From Pontiac, Michigan, take Michigan 59 West to Williams Lake Road and turn right. Turn left again at Gale Road. The trail begins at the beach parking lot on the left side of Gale Road. For information call (810) 666-1020. *DeLorme: Michigan Atlas & Gazetteer*: Page 41, C-6

(O) Potowatami, Michigan

Lots of people from the Toledo area head to the Potowatami Trail to get their singletrack fix. The Michigan Mountain Bike Association has done an excellent job of maintaining this trail. The rolling hills make for some fast riding, with short climbs and fast descents. There are plenty of drop-offs and sand sections to keep things technical.

From Ann Arbor, Michigan, take U.S. Route 23 North. Exit at North Territorial Road and go west about 10 miles. Turn right at Dexter-Townhall Road, and then right at Silver Hill Road. Park at Silver Lake Beach, where the trail starts. The park requires a $3 fee per car, but you get a map for that small fee. For information call (313) 426-4913. *DeLorme: Michgan Atlas & Gazetteer*: Page 32, A-2

Ⓟ Handlebar Hollow

With the help of the Hancock Handlebars Bicycle Club the city of Findlay, about an hour south of Toledo, has its own mountain bike trail. The mountain bike specific trail is only about two miles but offers some good riding for elevation-challenged Northwest Ohio. Sections of the trail are creatively named, such as Devil's Hole, The Snake, and Thunder Hollow.

From I-75 in Findlay, take West Trenton east. Turn right on Broad Street, then left on Howard. Turn right on Fox and park at the trailhead. For more information call the Hancock Park District at (419) 424-7176. *DeLorme: Ohio Atlas & Gazetteer:* Page 36, D-3

For those who have the inclination to race, there are events held almost every weekend in the Buckeye State. Many of these courses feature some of the best riding in the state. Unfortunately, some of these trails are only open to the riding public on race days.

Di Di Mau
Nelsonville, Ohio

This spring classic is one of the best and most trying races in the state. It attracts riders from all over the region, including pros like Floyd Landis, Kyle Dixon, and Gunner Shogren. The prizes are excellent and the course is very tough, especially when it is muddy. By the way, the nickname for this race is "The Mudder of all Races," due to its proximity to Mother's Day and the likelihood of encountering knee-deep mud. NORBA sanctioned. This trail is open for racing only.

The race is held on the campus of Hocking College. From Nelsonville go south on U.S. Route 33 then turn right on Ohio 691. Turn right at the sign for Hocking College. For information call (740) 698-4007.

Velo-Z
Duncan Falls, Ohio

One of the best, one of the first. Tom Hayes has developed one of the best race series in the state, with a fast, fun course and excellent prizes. This trail is open for racing only. Call Tom about camping before races at (614) 674-4297.

From Duncan Falls head south on Ohio 60 for about two miles. Tom Hayes' driveway is on the left, across from a sign on a telephone pole. It's easy to miss. The race starts at the top of the hill by the barn.

King's Domain Camp
Lebanon, Ohio

This is a three-mile course designed by Health and Fitness Promotions, who hold mountain bike and multi-sport races. This course features "lung burning climbs and death-hurling descents," according to the promoters. There is also a downhill race. NORBA sanctioned. For information call Health and Fitness Promotions at (614) 470-3988 or visit www.hfpracing.com.

Tappan Lake Park
Deersville, Ohio

Another Health and Fitness Promotions race, Tappan Lake features riding similar to Atwood Lake. This race also features a downhill and dual slalom. NORBA sanctioned. For information call Health and Fitness Promotions at (614) 470-3988 or visit www.hfpracing.com.

From Cleveland: Take Interstate 77 south to the U.S. Route 250 exit. Go east (left) on U.S. Route 250. Turn left at the Tappan Lake main entrance. It is well marked.

Clearfork Ski Resort
Butler, Ohio

This is the last race of the season for the Health and Fitness Promotions gurus. The course features lots of riding on the slopes as well as some woods riding for the singletrack sluts. This race also features a downhill and dual slalom. NORBA sanctioned. For information call Health and Fitness Promotions at (614) 470-3988 or visit www.hfpracing.com.

From Columbus: Take Interstate 71 north to Ohio 97. Take Ohio 97 east to Bellville. In Bellville go left (east) on Ohio 95. About 0.5 miles past Butler is Clear Fork Ski Resort.

Ohio Dirt Criterium Series
Mansfield, Ohio

The Dirt Criterium Series is a circuit race for mountain bikes, similar to a road criterium, but with tabletop jumps thrown in. This series runs in the winter so come prepared for cold, wet, and very muddy conditions. For information call Health and Fitness Promotions at (614) 470-3988 or visit www.hfpracing.com.

From Columbus- Take Interstate 71 north to the Mansfield / Lucas exit. Go left on Ohio 39 and drive about a quarter-mile. Turn right on Mt. Zion Road. Take Mt. Zion Road one mile and then turn right on Wallace Road. The Hock MTB Farm is on the left.

Bike Butler

Carrollton, Kentucky

General Butler State Park in Carrollton, Kentucky is home to one of the hardest races in the Ohio Valley. The course has numerous steep climbs and root-filled descents that allow little recovery. The park has first class amenities.

From Cincinnati: Take Interstate 71 south to Exit 44 (about 55 miles south of Cincinnati) and turn right on Kentucky 227 North. Go 1.5 miles to General Butler State Resort Park.

Other Race Locations In Ohio:

Hueston Woods State Park (see Ride 3)
Alum Creek State Park (see Ride 4)
Mickey's Mountain (see Ride 17)
Jefferson Lake State Park (see Ride 19)
Atwood Lake Park (see Ride 21)
Alpine Valley (see Ride 24)
Vulture's Knob (see Ride 25)
Mohican Wilderness (see Ride 26)

Appendix

Bicycle Clubs and Organizations

Local Clubs

Akron Bicycling Club
Stow, OH. A not-for-profit organization providing weekly social rides for riders of all abilities.
www.geocities.com/yosemite/7753

Bike Miami Valley
Dayton, OH. Bicycling advocacy group with extensive information on trails, organizations, and bicycling news.
www.bikemiamivalley.org
mailing list: www.listbot.com/bmv

Cincinnati Cycle Club
Milford, OH. Recreational and sport club for new and experienced riders on weekly rides year-round. www.cincinnaticycleclub.org

Cleveland Touring Club
Cleveland Heights, OH. Recreational cycling club for riders of all ages and abilities with weekly loop rides as well as special events and festival rides. www.clevetourclub.org

Columbus Outdoor Pursuits
Columbus, OH. A nonprofit organization providing outdoor recreation opportunities and training for youths and adults of Central Ohio.
www.on2morning.com/cop/

Crooked River Cyclists
Cleveland, OH. A USCF affiliated group in connection with the Crank Mail bicycling informational magazine serving the Greater Cleveland area. www.crankmail.com

Dayton Cycling Club (DCC)
Dayton, OH. A USCF and OBF, nonprofit educational and recreational organization for bicycle touring and racing in the Miami Valley.
www.daytoncyclingclub.org

Greater Ohioan Area Tandem Society (GOATS)
Cincinnati, OH. A social organization for tandem bike riders to share skills, information, and fun. Sponsors of the annual Miami Valley Tandem Rally. www.cinti.net/~gdbout/goats.htm

Heart of Ohio Tailwinds Bicycle Club
Marion, OH. Sponsors of the annual HOT Tamale race, and providers of weekly rides for bicyclists of all ability levels.
http://home1.gte.net/danshel/index.html

Lake Erie Wheelers
Lakewood, OH. Bicycling club for riders on the west side of Cleveland interested in many facets of biking such as touring, recreation, fitness, mountain biking, and racing.
www.geocities.com/Yosemite/Trails/2665

Maumee Valley Wheelmen
Perrysburg, OH. Toledo Area Bicycle Racing Club affiliated with USCF. Any can ride but only members can race. www.freewheel.com/index.html

Miami Valley Rail Trails
Dayton, OH. Part of the Rails-to-Trails Conservancy, this group provides information on available rail trails in Southwest Ohio.
www.intellweb.com/trails

Ohio Bicycle Federation
Vandalia, OH. Alliance of individuals and organizations to promote the use of bicycles for recreation, transportation, and provide opportunities for the betterment of bicycle education, engineering, and legislation.
www.ohiobike.org

Queen City Wheels
Loveland, OH. A member club of USA Cycling, promoting sanctioned bicycle racing in the greater Cincinnati area. For information hotline: (513) 682-9292. http://qcw.org

Stark County Bicycle Club

Canton, OH. Club for Northeastern Ohio comprised of all types of bikers. Monthly newsletter with current information on rides and races. http://members.aol.com/starkscbc/scbc

Westerville Bicycle Club

Westerville, OH. Central Ohio's nonprofit, recreational and touring club for bicyclists of all ages and abilities. www.westervillebicycleclub.org

National Clubs and Organizations

American Trails

The only national, nonprofit organization working on behalf of ALL trail interests. Members want to create and protect America's network of interconnected trailways.
POB 200787
Denver, CO 80220
(303) 321-6606
www.outdoorlink.com/amtrails

International Mountain Bicycling Association

(IMBA) Works to keep public lands accessible to bikers and provides information of trail design and maintenance.
POB 7578
Boulder, CO 80306
(303) 545-9011, www.greatoutdoors.com/imba

National Off-Road Bicycling Association

(NORBA) National governing body of US mountain bike racing.
One Olympic Plaza
Colorado Springs, CO 80909
(719) 578-4717, www.usacycling.org/mtb

Outdoor Recreation Coalition of America

(ORCA) Oversees and examines issues for outdoor recreation
Boulder, CO
(303) 444-3353
www.orca.org
info@orca.org

Rails-to-Trails Conservancy

Organized to promote conversion of abandoned rail corridors to trails for public use.
1400 16th Street, NW, Suite 300
Washington, D.C. 20036-2222
www.railtrails.org

League of American Wheelmen

190 West Ostend Street #120
Baltimore, MD 21230-3731
(410) 539-3399

United States Cycling Federation

Governing body for amateur cycling.
Colorado Springs, CO
(719) 578-4581
www.usacycling.org

USA Cycling

One Olympic Plaza
Colorado Springs, CO 80909
(719) 578-4581
www.usacycling.org

Dear Reader: *It's the very nature of print media that the second the presses run off the last book, all the phone numbers change. If you notice a wrong number or that a club or organization has disappeared or that a new one has put out its shingle, we'd love to know about it. And if you run a club or have a favorite one and we missed it; again, let us know. We plan on doing our part to keep this list up-to-date for future editions, but we could always use the help. You can write us, call us, e-mail us, or heck, just stop by if you're in the neighborhood.*

Outside America
300 West Main Street, Suite A
Charlottesville, Virginia 22903
(804) 245-6800
editorial@outside-america.com

Fat Tire Vacations

[Bicycle Touring Companies]

There are literally dozens of off-road bicycling tour companies offering an incredible variety of guided tours for mountain bikers. On these pay-as-you-pedal, fat-tire vacations, you will have a chance to go places around the globe that only an expert can take you, and your experiences will be so much different than if seen through the window of a tour bus.

From Hut to Hut in the Colorado Rockies or Inn to Inn through Vermont's Green Mountains, there is a tour company for you. Whether you want hardcore singletrack during the day and camping at night, or you want scenic trails followed by a bottle of wine at night and a mint on each pillow, someone out there offers what you're looking for. The tours are well organized and fully supported with expert guides, bike mechanics, and "sag wagons" which carry gear, food, and tired bodies. Prices range from $100-$500 for a weekend to more than $2000 for two-week-long trips to far-off lands such as New Zealand or Ireland. Each of these companies will gladly send you their free literature to whet your appetite with breathtaking photography and titillating stories of each of their tours.

Vacations

Selected Touring Companies

Elk River Touring Center
Slatyfork, WV
(304) 572-3771

Vermont Bicycling Touring
Bristol, VT
1-800-245-3868

Backroads
Berkley, CA
1-800-BIKE TRIP

Timberline Bicycle Tours
Denver, CO
(303) 759-3804

Roads Less Traveled
Longmont, CO
(303) 678-8750

Blackwater Bikes
Davis, WV
(304) 259-5286

Bicycle Adventures
Olympia, WA
1-800-443-6060

Trails Unlimited, Inc.
Nashville, IN
(812) 988-6232

Repair and Mainten

FIXING A FLAT

TOOLS YOU WILL NEED

- Two tire irons
- Pump (either a floor pump or a frame pump)
- No screwdrivers!!! (This can puncture the tube)

REMOVING THE WHEEL

The front wheel is easy. Simply open the quick release mechanism or undo the bolts with the proper sized wrench, then remove the wheel from the bike.

The rear wheel is a little more tricky. Before you loosen the wheel from the frame, shift the chain into the smallest gear on the freewheel (the cluster of gears in the back). Once you've done this, removing and installing the wheel, like the front, is much easier.

REMOVING THE TIRE

Step one: Insert a tire iron under the bead of the tire and pry the tire over the lip of the rim. Be careful not to pinch the tube when you do this.

Step two: Hold the first tire iron in place. With the second tire iron, repeat step one, three or four inches down the rim. Alternate tire irons, pulling the bead of the tire over the rim, section by section, until one side of the tire bead is completely off the rim.

Step three: Remove the rest of the tire and tube from the rim. This can be done by hand. It's easiest to remove the valve stem last. Once the tire is off the rim, pull the tubeout of the tire.

CLEAN AND SAFETY CHECK

Step four: Using a rag, wipe the inside of the tire to clean out any dirt, sand, glass, thorns, etc. These may cause the tube to puncture. The inside of a tire should feel smooth. Any pricks or bumps could mean that you have found the culprit responsible for your flat tire.

Step five: Wipe the rim clean, then check the rim strip, making sure it covers the spoke nipples properly on the inside of the rim. If a spoke is poking through the rim strip, it could cause a puncture.

Step six: At this point, you can do one of two things: replace the punctured tube with a new one, or patch the hole. It's easiest to just replace the tube with a new tube when you're out on the trails. Roll up the old tube and take it home to repair later that night in front of the TV. Directions on patching a tube are usually included with the patch kit itself.

INSTALLING THE TIRE AND TUBE
(This can be done entirely by hand)

Step seven: Inflate the new or repaired tube with enough air to give it shape, then tuck it back into the tire.

Step eight: To put the tire and tube back on the rim, begin by putting the valve in the valve hole. The valve must be straight. Then use your hands to push the beaded edge of the tire onto the rim all the way around so that one side of your tire is on the rim.

Step nine: Let most of the air out of the tube to allow room for the rest of the tire.

Step ten: Beginning opposite the valve, use your thumbs to push the other side of the tire onto the rim. Be careful not to pinch the tube in between the tire and the rim. The last few inches may be difficult, and you may need the tire iron to pry the tire onto the rim. If so, just be careful not to puncture the tube.

BEFORE INFLATING COMPLETELY

Step eleven: Check to make sure the tire is seated properly and that the tube is not caught between the tire and the rim. Do this by adding about 5 to 10 pounds of air, and watch closely that the tube does not bulge out of the tire.

Step twelve: Once you're sure the tire and tube are properly seated, put the wheel back on the bike, then fill the tire with air. It's easier squeezing the wheel through the brake shoes if the tire is still flat.

Step thirteen: Now fill the tire with the proper amount of air, and check constantly to make sure the tube doesn't bulge from the rim. If the tube does appear to bulge out, release all the air as quickly as possible, or you could be in for a big bang.

When installing the rear wheel, place the chain back onto the smallest cog (furthest gear on the right), and pull the derailleur out of the way. Your wheel should slide right on.

LUBRICATION PREVENTS DETERIORATION

Lubrication is crucial to maintaining your bike. Dry spots will be eliminated. Creaks, squeaks, grinding, and binding will be gone. The chain will run quietly, and the gears will shift smoothly. The brakes will grip quicker, and your bike may last longer with fewer repairs. Need I say more? Well, yes. Without knowing where to put the lubrication, what good is it?

THINGS YOU WILL NEED
- One can of bicycle lubricant, found at any bike store.
- A clean rag (to wipe excess lubricant away).

WHAT GETS LUBRICATED
- Front derailleur
- Rear derailleur
- Shift levers
- Front brake
- Rear brake
- Both brake levers
- Chain

WHERE TO LUBRICATE

To make it easy, simply spray a little lubricant on all the pivot points of your bike. If you're using a squeeze bottle, use just a drop or two. Put a few drops on each point wherever metal moves against metal, for instance, at the center of the brake calipers. Then let the lube sink in.

Once you have applied the lubricant to the derailleurs, shift the gears a few times, working the derailleurs back and forth. This allows the lubricant to work itself into the tiny cracks and spaces it must occupy to do its job. Work the brakes a few times as well.

LUBING THE CHAIN

Lubricating the chain should be done after the chain has been wiped clean of most road grime. Do this by spinning the pedals counterclockwise while gripping the chain with a clean rag. As you add the lubricant, be sure to get some in between each link. With an aerosol spray, just spray the chain while pedalling backwards (counterclockwise) until the chain is fully lubricated. Let the lubricant soak in for a few seconds before wiping the excess away. Chains will collect dirt much faster if they're loaded with too much lubrication.

Index

Index

F

G

H

I

J

K

L

M

Euphoria...
in many different states.

The most beautiful, challenging and exhilarating rides are just a day-trip away.

Visit **www.outside-america.com** *to order the latest guides for areas near you – or not so near. Also, get information and updates on future publications and other guidebooks from Outside America™.*

For more information or to place an order, Call **1-800-243-0495.**

Meet the Author

Adam Vincent got his first taste of singletrack as a grade-schooler in the woods near his house in Northwest Ohio. After a brief stint as a roadie, he began mountain biking seriously while attending Ohio University. When not studying for his journalism degree, he rode the steep hilly trails and gravel roads of Southern Ohio. His passion for both riding and writing led him to an internship at *Mountain Bike* magazine. After graduation he sold and wrenched on bikes at Century Cycles in Medina, Ohio. Today he's an associate editor for the trade magazine *Bicycle Retailer & Industry News*.

Author